VISIBLE MEN

MANIFESTING CHRIST IN MARRIAGE

ANTONE M. GOYAK

Edited by: Sarah Hayhurst Editorial, Inc.

Cover and layout design: Author Brand Studio

Independently published

ISBN: 9781729387917

To my sweet love and best friend Stefanie. You were the catalyst for this amazing journey. You were my cheerleader, confidant, sounding board, and gracious critic. This book is our marriage on display and though not always pretty, it is a narrative of the gospel at work in two lives. And reading it only reminds me of the kindness and grace that Jesus has showed to us in our brokenness. I love you and I know you love me.

CONTENTS

FOREWORD

We are all broken. Our best efforts in marriage, family, and extended relationships starkly reveal the battle scars of brokenness. This fractured state is the starting point to both victorious living and ministry effectiveness. When we begin to understand our spiritual deficiency and dire need for the gospel, we can better envision God's strength made perfect in weakness. It is only through his divine intervention and guidance that good and lasting works can be accomplished.

Marriage, in particular, shines a glaring light on our inadequacies. A mismanaged, hurting relationship can hide deep in the crevices of prideful and pretentious living. While others may extend praiseworthy comments toward the *perfect couple,* in reality there may be an abundance of tension and stress lurking behind the flimsy facade. What looks good on the outside is often rotten to the core.

Marriage is far more than a commitment and a ring: it is a magnificent yet strenuous work in progress. Over time, *love, honor, and cherish* can soon become lost on the rabbit trails of busyness and send one life path into two different directions. As seen in the pages of this book, even successful men of integrity and purpose can lose their way. It is important to note that seeking accountability, transparency, and wise counsel from likeminded men of God are key tools to maintaining biblical perspective.

Several years ago we embarked on a family vacation to Disney World. My wife claims it was anything but a *family* adventure. Following each thrill, show, or event, my Indiana Jones personality was off to explore the next best option with the shortest line. According to my beloved, I was always thirty feet ahead "cutting down the weeds!"

Such is the story of many men. We plow ahead with responsibilities, checklists, and a predetermined agenda while cluelessly leaving our dear wife behind to fend for herself. We work on *our* dreams and forget about hers, on *our* plans and desires rather than painting a splendid canvas together. The outcome is a frustrating puzzle with numerous missing pieces. At best, we exist!

Antone Goyak has written a wake-up call to men with noble ideals and good intentions. He humbly exposes his own missteps through a beautiful marriage and the training of three godly, servant-minded kids. As dear brothers in Christ, we have enjoyed some of that journey together, challenging one another to set the leadership bar high and to continuously find the heartbeat of the wives of our youth.

I entreat you to carefully read these pages with an open mind and heart … not merely as instruction and guidance for others. Allow God to speak to you through the experience of a co-laborer but primarily through the living Word of our Almighty Counselor. Surround your wife with God's love and learn to enjoy life in tandem, smoothly taking each step together in obedience to the covenant you once made before God and witnesses.

—Chaplain Hugh McCoy, DMin

PREFACE

It all began our freshman year of college. He was from California and I from Florida. He was quiet. And me? Well, not so much. We began our journey of dating in 1984 to now being married twenty-nine years. We have lived many beautiful moments, but our marriage has been far from a bed of roses. My love for this man has not diminished but has actually grown exponentially.

As Antone began to get in community with other men, both single and married, the desire to share the workings of God through his own brokenness became a reoccurring point of conversation. Thus, the birth of "writing it down" began, and yes, telling his story to the world started to unfold.

The reality of what my husband began to expose was a bit daunting. Antone's desire was not to make this book about himself (or us) but rather about the transforming work of a loving and holy God. He, without apology, wants to point this story to King Jesus—the one who has unlimited grace, mercy, and forgiveness, which he desires to bestow on those he created in his image.

As Antone and I engage in marriage counseling sessions or have dinner with another couple who is looking for hope and the fortitude to just keep going on, Antone's admonition is not to try harder or do more but to focus on a proper view of God.

This man, my precious husband and friend and the mentor of many, has a transformed heart only by God's doing. I not only have had the opportunity to observe the transformation but also have reaped the spiritual fruit that accompanies a genuine and forever change.

To God be the glory, great things He has done (1 Chronicles 16:8–34).

—Stefanie Goyak

ACKNOWLEDGEMENTS

I have found that writing my first book is much like a marriage: you never truly begin to understand its foundational elements until you are actually immersed in it. There is a large chasm between what I thought writing a book would look like and what it ended up being for me.

It is only fitting and appropriate to begin this book by making much of those who influenced what might have been good to make it immeasurably better in its content, richer in its thoughts, and clearer in its design.

I want to thank my Savior, Jesus, for giving me a view of marriage that I could have never obtained myself. You both restored and redeemed my relationship to Stefanie and gave me joy that I never knew to be possible. You changed my heart—a work I could have never done. I am overwhelmed, humbled, and grateful.

To my sweet wife: you are the only person who has chosen to live this journey with me. It means the world that you support the content of this book. You have experienced my brokenness in marriage and have chosen to overflow grace and forgiveness along the way. Thank you for your endearing love, friendship, commitment, and the oneness we enjoy. God has used our valleys to put us in a season of marriage that I hope never ends. You are amazingly wonderful, and I love you.

To all of my family: your words of encouragement helped to provide motivation and discipline to stick with this dream of mine and finish what I had started. I am grateful for you. Your feedback is important to me.

My friends who reviewed my manuscript: I love you guys and am so appreciative for your insights and wisdom. To Alex Tunnicliff: thank you for shaping my book to keep it gospel centric; to Jack Ambrosius, Luke Vandergriff, Bobby Wood, Ben Wilhite, Hugh McCoy, Greg Books, Matt Olson, and Ron Wolfe: I so appreciate your not only reading my book but offering me valuable feedback to make it stronger and more relevant; to Steve Whigham: your early advice and ideas of getting this work off the ground were timely and put to use; to Doug McDowell and Steve Nooyen: your partnership with me in my book project has been humbling and an incredible blessing. In addition, Steve, your cabin in the woods was so helpful in collecting and drafting my thoughts on this book over the days I stayed there. Thank you for your generosity.

Finally, I am very thankful for Sarah Hayhurst for her role in editing my book. You provided such helpful expertise and suggestions that gave me much confidence in my work. And to Michael and Amy Kuo of Author Brand Studio: you both have been amazing to work with, and I appreciate your creativity and desire to turn my manuscript into something that overflows who I am. You are great cheerleaders.

INTRODUCTION

"I do."

"I. Do."

I remember speaking these words as if I spoke them yesterday. But it wasn't yesterday. It was over twenty-nine years ago. And not just to any woman. *My* woman.

I can see her walking down the decorated aisle with her soft red hair and stunning white dress—the very center of all beauty that day.

She. Looked. Magnificent.

I do not recall the exact thought I had, but it was something to the effect of *Oh, my word.* I know, not the most poetic response, but at twenty-three years of age, *this woman,* who was soon to become *my wife,* took not only my breath away but also every coherent thought.

"I do." To be completely honest, the rest of the ceremony was somewhat of a blur. I really did not care what the pastor asked me with regard to *this woman,* I was going to agree.

"Antone, do you take this woman to be your wife, to live together in holy marriage? Do you promise to love her, comfort her, honor, and keep her in sickness and in health, and forsaking all others, be faithful to her as long as you both shall live?"

And as the pastor paused to wait for my response, I looked directly into the beautiful eyes of my bride and said with confidence, "I do." To love, to comfort, to honor, to keep, to forsake all others *for her*. But did I comprehend the depth and breadth of my response? Did it resonate that I was making a *covenantal vow?*

In a word, "no." Has *any* husband fully grasped the gravity of his promise on the day he was married? Our premarital counseling consisted of a twenty-minute meeting with my wife's pastor the week of our marriage. I was good to go.

Or so I thought.

As our marriage unfolded into years, I expected that becoming a "godly husband" would come naturally.

But then life happened.

I convinced myself all was well, but it was in those dark, honest moments I realized that I was ill-equipped to lead my bride. Even though I loved her, I found within me selfish desires, a rebel heart, and crushing brokenness. And what about other guys? Did they struggle being godly husbands? Did they wrestle with these same thoughts? Our unwritten "guy code" taught us not to dive into these topics. Everything was "fine." Always "fine," as sports and small talk hijacked deeper conversations.

I could manage work. I could manage my home. But I could not manage my marriage because it was never meant to be managed. And though Ephesians 5:25 rolled off my tongue with ease, it betrayed my hidden fears within my insecure heart. Pursuing my wife like *Jesus pursues his church* seemed like a lofty metaphor that was impossible to experience.

So, God began a process of breaking and remaking me. And the very gospel that transformed my heart as a follower of Jesus Christ was the same gospel God employed in transforming my marriage.

And he did. Radically.

I know too many guys who lose hope in their marriages because the ritualistic staleness, daily chaos, or inner conflict seem insurmountable, and so they disengage. And as their wives cry out for the hearts of their husbands, they either don't know how to change, or they get preoccupied and overlook their wives' longings altogether. Oh sure, they still live in domestic relationships, but their hearts are universes apart.

If this describes you as a husband, then be encouraged, for this is a story of great hope. Because after twenty-nine years of marriage, I am experiencing more joy and intimacy than any other time. And at the age of fifty-two, I am in a season of life where I have increased influence with men. This is not about giving myself accolades; rather, it is a compelling desire to tell my story about God aligning my marriage with his gospel in spite of my poor efforts. It is about my surprising journey of heart change within a relationship called marriage.

And so comes the title for this book: *Visible Men*. By being a visible man, I am not urging us as husbands to show up more in our marriages. You know, be more present, do things for your wife, be with her more often, or her seeing you are "there." The key is not a "what" but a "who." The subtitle of my book describes the visible husband: *Manifesting Christ in Marriage*. The staleness and dysfunctionality that I have experienced in my marriage came because of an identity crisis: I was more concerned about my agenda, my purposes, and my image being visible in my marriage than about Jesus being visible. To "manifest" means something is readily perceived, evident, obvious, or apparent. My journey through marriage in recent years has been exactly this concept. As God changed my heart and its very affections, I did not have to say to my wife, "Hey, babe, look! I am modeling Jesus for you!" No, rather it was quite evident and apparent to her that something was different in how I was loving her in our marriage. To be a visible man in your marriage means it is both obvious and evident to your wife that the gospel has gripped and owns your heart. *A* bridegroom is now manifesting *the* Bridegroom. Jesus is made known.

This book is designed to engage you in your thoughts and spirit. To that end, you will find *So here is what you should be asking* … at the end of each chapter. Each is comprised of three questions:

- Communion with God, designed for self-reflection in one key principle from the chapter.
- Communication with your wife, designed to engage you in healthy conversation with your wife about a key area from the chapter. If your marriage is going to look like Jesus, you must involve your wife in God's process of your sanctification.
- Community with other men, designed to make you comfortable in talking with other men about your brokenness and the hope found only in Jesus.

I would encourage you to make working through these questions as relevant as reading the text. They will help you come to gospel conclusions.

When you smash your finger with a hammer for the tenth time, you start to learn both what *to* do and what *not* to do. God teaches through life, and he is an amazingly patient and skilled artisan. But rest assured, this is not about your doing more, trying harder, or "fixing" your life. It is simply about the transformative power of King Jesus in your marriage and being visible men.

CHAPTER 1

IN FULL PURSUIT

I have never met another husband who claims to be a follower of Jesus who also sets out to have a reckless or disappointing marriage. I cannot think of one instance. I have never had a conversation with one, who claims King Jesus, who mapped out a planned rut for his relationship with his wife. Though I have tried, nothing comes to mind.

Why does there seem to be such a pandemic sweeping through marriages? I talk with a lot of married men, and over time transparent conversations begin to emerge about their failing marriages. And as I listen, I usually hear one of two scenarios.

The first scenario is the admission of guilt but with the greater blame placed on the wife.

"Yeah, I know I should lead and love my wife, but do you know how she treats me?"

"If she would only stop doing (whatever), it would allow me to be a better leader."

"My wife is so frustrating and demanding sometimes! What am I supposed to do?"

Enter Sean. (Names have been changed to protect the guilty!)

I have known Sean for a while. He is married with kids, and his marriage is a disaster, living together yet hearts far apart. Despite his seeking out pornography and emotionally stiff-arming his wife, he still readily places blame on her and criticizes her lack of love toward him. I have laid out the beauty of the gospel, but *his* "beauty" seems more appealing. We talk, a spark seems to ignite, but nothing ever seems to change.

In the second scenario, I am hearing guys say they really *do* want better marriages. They *want* to change. They *need* to change. They admit that they are poorly leading and loving. But nothing ever *seems* to change.

Enter Patrick.

I really enjoy being around him. Just a good, all-around guy from the surface. But his marriage is stale. His wife is frustrated that he is aloof about their marriage. She is just not in his "crosshairs," and he is content with the status quo. She readily recalls the exact number of days it has been since he last said, "I love you." He knows and admits there is a problem and wants things to be different. I have laid out multiple strategies for him. Resolve strengthens for a time but then wanes. And what is supposed to be a beautiful picture is simply another stale relationship, featuring a frustrated husband and a discouraged wife. Nothing ever seems to change.

These are two accounts that I have unfolded, and yet there are many others that could be told. But each sad story is familiar: no full pursuit of a bride.

It is essential early on to establish what I mean by the phrase "in full pursuit." You may have your own mental image in mind, but I want to craft a very specific definition so that we hit the bullseye of a very biblical target.

A STORY OF PURSUIT

You are not going to find the phrase "in full pursuit" anywhere in Scripture though the imagery is very much present. It is meant to cause me to contemplate the faithful, sacrificial, and redemptive love my Savior has for me as his bride. It is a picture, one that does not require excess or lofty words to capture its full meaning.

It simply stands on its own.

But I am going to help us grasp "in full pursuit" by telling you a true story about John and Laura. This couple has a very unique narrative, one you are not going to hear every day. John and Laura get married, and life begins like any other marriage. And they were not too far into their marriage before their first child was born, then another, and finally a third. Two boys and a little girl. Family life was going well, or so it seemed.

What you don't know about this couple is the very different walks of life that each brought into this marriage. John was a follower of Jesus early on and felt the calling of God on his life. Laura came from what you might call an "alternate lifestyle."

She had been a prostitute.

She had given herself for the pleasure of others for a price. In a very unusual twist to the story, she came out of prostitution and ended up marrying John. Old life forsaken. New life embraced.

Sometime after their third child was born, John noticed that Laura seemed a bit distant. She always seemed to have a quick response, but details were not matching up. Things finally came to a head when a friend confided in John that he had seen Laura with another man.

Another man? He was sick to his stomach.

It was not too long before the sordid details came out, and John discovered to his horror that, not only was Laura being unfaithful to their marriage, she was once again in the throes of selling her body for sex. His wife was absent, physically and spiritually, and a mother had abandoned her children for mere pleasure. He began to wonder if any of his children were not really his.

John's spirit was crushed to the very core, and his mind was reeling. His grief and heartache over his bride were almost too much to bear. The bitterness, anger, and despair were like strong hands choking the life out of him. *Why?* He would view his favorite picture of his wife and him and sob uncontrollably. Why would she go back to this? Was he not a good enough husband? Did he do something that pushed her away? He still loved her, but she seemingly no longer loved him. Did she still love him? John felt shackled by his own emotions and took solace in solitude.

But God was a faithful Father and overflowed his mercy to this broken man. His overwhelming grace, his steadfast love, his far-as-the-east-is-from-the-west forgiveness. And John was not so quick to forsake the covenant with his wife as she did. And one evening, in a most surprising turn of events, John left his house and took one step out the door. And then another. And another. He wandered through his city from person to person, house to house, and friend to friend, asking if anyone had seen his beloved.

After a few days, he found her living in her prostitution once again. And she was with *another* man, her "lover." Her eyes were unable to meet his staring longingly at her. Lovingly. Forgivingly. He still loved this woman who was now lusted after by another man. But she did not belong to *this other* man, for she was *his* wife. He, and not this other man, made a covenantal vow to this woman. They had given themselves to each other.

But if John wanted her back, it would cost him money, he was told. *Money?* What kind of perversion was this? And though he owed this other man *nothing,* he willingly paid to buy back what was already his. For she was his wife even though she had been an adulteress. And even though *she left him, he went after her* because he loved her because she was his.

And she began to weep. And she sobbed uncontrollably.

And overwhelmed by this kind of other-worldly love, this redeeming love, Laura willingly went back home to John and her family. And they rebuilt their broken marriage one day at a time.

For she had been pursued.

GOD THE COSMIC PURSUER

As I said at the beginning, this is a true account. Perhaps not modern-day, but true nonetheless. It actually comes from the Old Testament book of Hosea. Israel has *the* true God, Jehovah, as their God. God was the ever-faithful bridegroom, and Israel was his bride. And God's first commandment, as given to Moses, lacked no clarity: "You shall have *no other* gods before me."

And yet they did. Israel found God to be tiring and distant and not as exciting as the gods of other lands. So, God came up with his own story to play out for the people. He tells Hosea the prophet to marry a prostitute named Gomer. Commentators offer differing views of whether Gomer was a woman with an immoral past or if she was actively engaged in prostitution. Regardless, she proves to be unfaithful to Hosea. And God does this to illustrate to Israel how she has played the harlot by forsaking the true God and turning to others.

Pretty radical.

It was meant to turn heads and cause people to stare. It was meant to create a stomach-churning disgust. It was meant to make a point. And as the story develops between Hosea and his wife, we see her leave her husband and her children and return to her former ways.

"So she has left! Divorce her!" you can hear the friends of Hosea argue. If not that, Hosea could have had her stoned based on Old Testament law. But he didn't. Because then God does the unthinkable. He says to Hosea, "Go and love your wife again, even though she commits adultery with another lover. This will illustrate that the LORD still loves Israel, even though the people have turned to other gods and love to worship them" (Hosea 3:1 NLT).

And Hosea goes. He finds this "significant other" and discovers *his wife* there with him. And the only way he can get her back is by making payment for her. *Payment?* How can you make payment for a woman who is already your wife? This just seems so, so wrong. But in order to have her delivered from her physical and spiritual slavery, he willingly secures her release.

And he brings her home to restore her as his wife.

If your reaction to this is "What?", it is the same as mine. How can this be? The Old Testament was very clear on the consequences of adultery, and now God is asking Hosea to chase after his wife and love her again?[1]

Understand this is not a story about Hosea being a remarkable husband. It is not a story about Hosea giving his wife a second chance. If we settle our conclusion there, we have missed the entire objective of the story. Rather, it is about the unfathomable attributes of Yahweh and his love and pursuit for his people. This is a story about *the* Bridegroom. Read the love song of God for his bride Israel even in the midst of their unfaithfulness:

> *Therefore, behold, I will allure her, and bring her into the wilderness, and speak tenderly to her. And there I will give her her vineyards and make the Valley of Achor a door of hope. And there she shall answer as in the days of her youth, as at the time when she came out of the land of Egypt.*

And in that day, declares the LORD, you will call me 'My Husband,' and no longer will you call me 'My Baal.' For I will remove the names of the Baals from her mouth, and they shall be remembered by name no more. And I will make for them a covenant on that day with the beasts of the field, the birds of the heavens, and the creeping things of the ground. And I will abolish the bow, the sword, and war from the land, and I will make you lie down in safety. And I will betroth you to me forever. I will betroth you to me in righteousness and in justice, in steadfast love and in mercy. I will betroth you to me in faithfulness. And you shall know the LORD.

And in that day I will answer, declares the LORD, I will answer the heavens, and they shall answer the earth, and the earth shall answer the grain, the wine, and the oil, and they shall answer Jezreel, and I will sow her for myself in the land. And I will have mercy on No Mercy, and I will say to Not My People, 'You are my people'; and he shall say, 'You are my God' (Hosea 2:14–23).

WHY THIS FIRST MUST BE ABOUT THE GOSPEL

Such a beautiful picture. Such steadfast love by a relentless God. And as I lay out the framework for this first chapter, I want to be clear from the onset that though this book is most certainly about your marriage, it first must be about the relationship *you* have with this covenant-keeping God and his gospel.

Just what do I mean by the word "gospel"? I resonate strongly with Tim Keller's definition: "The gospel is this: We are more sinful and flawed in ourselves than we ever dared believe, yet at the very same time we are more loved and accepted in Jesus Christ than we ever dared hope."[2]

The truth of the matter is that I need a savior and I make a horrible one. But Jesus is better. And if you and I do not have an active and redemptive gospel presence in our lives, our marriages will always be something less than they could be. In fact, they will fail, and you will rob God of his glory. The gospel rescues us from ourselves. When my heart wants its own way, its own passions, and its own desires, the gospel counters this not with behavior management but with genuine heart change. Go ahead, try to clean up yourself and your marriage by trying harder or being more diligent. Try to change your heart posture or longings. You cannot do it. It may last for a while, but it will be temporary. And like me, you will end up deeper in the hole of your own making.

God and his gospel counter our efforts by offering *life* through his process of sanctification. Jesus offers *his* strength in exchange for our weakness. He offers *his* love in place of our lust. He gladly gives *his* patience for our own frustrations. He gives us his Word to shape our thoughts and desires. He frees us from our slavery to sin and to ourselves and adopts us as sons.

You must not miss this for it is the key to every chapter in this book. "In him" the apostle Paul declares throughout the New Testament (Ephesians 1). Manifesting Jesus in your life is your only hope to be the man your wife needs. And manifesting Jesus in your marriage is your only hope for a thriving marriage that brings glory to God. Jesus is not an add-on, and he does not simply provide assistance when needed. Our brokenness must cry out as a longing of dependence for him.

WHAT IT MEANS TO PURSUE MY WIFE

I have thought long and hard on this phrase "in full pursuit," and its meaning goes far deeper for me when held in the light of this story in Hosea. It is an amazing picture, an *impossible* picture, but yet one I am trying to wrap my thoughts around.

Not too long ago my wife and I drove our daughter to her university to begin her second year of school. Our car was so packed with all of her necessities that maybe, *just maybe,* we could have squeezed in another pair of socks, but they would have only fit in the freezer section of her portable refrigerator.

Sometime during the course of that day, I was thinking about "in full pursuit" and drafted some notes on my phone. As my wife and I were driving home that evening, we spent some time talking about what it means for a man to pursue, or chase after, his wife. I had some initial thoughts I wanted her to read from my phone, and we went back and forth on the words required to picture such a definition. It was very helpful to hear her feedback.

And as we talked, I gained more clarity as I began to listen to her heart's perspective. And this where I landed: *To pursue my wife is to intentionally cultivate, lead, and serve her in a redemptive manner as I will give an account as a loving steward in presenting her to King Jesus.*

The *how* of this definition is of greatest importance and where I want to initially focus. I cultivate, lead, and serve my wife in a *redemptive* manner. In other words, I make the most of every opportunity, turning each to her best advantage since none can be recalled if overlooked or cast away.[3]

The *why* of this definition is something we as guys do not contemplate as much as we ought. I do not pursue my wife primarily to maintain unity, though that is an important consideration. I do not pursue my wife just for sexual intimacy, though certainly that is an amazing gift of God.

The primary reason I pursue or chase after my bride is for the glory of God (1 Corinthians 10:31). In properly reflecting the gospel, there is a *responsibility* I have before God that I took on when I uttered the words "I do." And the accountability placed before me is that I am stewarding the livelihood of my wife, both physically and spiritually. That as a daughter of the High King, I am spending my time in marriage readying her for her bridegroom, Jesus Christ.

That is what a steward does. He manages or cares for something or someone placed in his charge. And the very act of being made a steward implies something about that person's character and motives. He only does for the glory of his master. He could use his position of authority to his own advantage, but his purpose is to protect and serve for the success of the one he serves.[4]

So too are we as husbands. We are to lovingly serve our wives for the glory of our master, King Jesus. But what I often miss as a husband is how my marriage is divinely designed to picture something greater and far loftier than a man and woman merely coexisting together.

It is meant to mirror another relationship—the relationship that Jesus, as the bridegroom, has with his church, the bride. And it is not just any relationship but one of service, sacrifice, and selflessness.

Husbands, love your wives, as Christ loved the church and gave himself up for her, that he might sanctify her, having cleansed her by the washing of water with the word, so that he might present the church to himself in splendor, without spot or wrinkle or any such thing, that she might be holy and without blemish (Ephesians 5:25–27).

So, if our earthly marriages were predetermined by God to represent a heavenly reality, allow me to pose a question to you. What would Christ's pursuit of the church look like if it mirrored *your* own marriage? In other words, what if the heavenly reality of covenantal love took form after your own covenantal love for your wife?

Reality check, huh? It was for me. And that question is not meant to craft a sense of guilt within you; rather, it is purposed to help you realize *what is at stake* with your own marriage. Guys, whether you agree or not or realize it or not, there is a rippling effect from how you pursue your wife. Your wife is influenced. Your kids are influenced. Your friends are influenced. Your church body is influenced. And above all, the furtherance of the gospel is influenced.

We do live not live life in a vacuum, men. Our marriages do not and cannot exist apart from the story that the rest of our lives are telling. And if your marriage is less than what I have described above, and if you believe it is "just the way it is" and that it can be offset by fulfillment in your job, distractions provided by your favorite hobby, or chasing after virtual women on the internet, you are sorely mistaken.

The truth is that if your wife is not sensing you are actively pursuing her in a biblical manner, you are distorting and perverting the lens through which others view the gospel of Jesus Christ. And more importantly, you are distorting and perverting the lens through which *your wife* is viewing Jesus and his love for her.

It's a heavy weight, isn't it? And though it is good to feel the weight of what the pursuit of your wife *actually means,* it was never meant for you to come up with a plan to fix things. You know, try harder. Do more. Be better.

The primary issue is not that we as husbands are lacking in our effort. Sure, that might be a by-product, but it is not *the* point in question. Your greatest need and my greatest need is an accurate view of God. For without an authentic and correct belief about the Father, Son, and Holy Spirit, my marriage will simply be a picture of my own sinful brokenness.

In other words, an epic fail.

Read this definition again: *To pursue my wife is to intentionally cultivate, lead, and serve her in a redemptive manner as I will give an account as a loving steward in presenting her to King Jesus.*

If you know you are not pursuing your wife like Jesus pursues his church, or if you know what your wife would say if you asked her, I want you to keep reading because there is hope. The same power of the gospel that has and is radically transforming my own heart is the same power that can radically transform yours.

We just need to recalibrate how we are viewing our God and how he is viewing each of us. Let's get started.

So here is what you should be asking . . .

COMMUNION WITH GOD: Review the definition in this chapter of what it means to pursue your wife. If you are completely honest in evaluating yourself, which element presents the biggest roadblock to you? Why? How can the power of the gospel counter this need?

COMMUNICATION WITH YOUR WIFE: Read the same definition to your wife. Ask her to communicate ways that make her feel pursued spiritually, physically, and emotionally.

COMMUNITY WITH OTHER MEN: Find someone who is displaying this type of pursuit with his wife. Ask him how he is finding success in biblically loving her.

CHAPTER 2

RECALIBRATING MY VIEW OF GOD

One of the most insightful quotes I have heard is one by A. W. Tozer when he said, "What comes into our minds when we think about God is the most important thing about us."[1]

As a guy I find it easy to compartmentalize my life. Like I have heard it said: we men are like waffles; women are like spaghetti. My wife is able to, in an uncanny way, see interrelationships between people and events and how the parts fit within the whole. She's the spaghetti, where any one person or circumstance is "touching many other noodles."

I, on the other hand, like to categorize my life into separate squares, like waffles. It keeps things uncomplicated and makes it easier to identify problems and solutions. But that mindset can easily lead to believing that other areas of my life can be kept separate—that one does not necessarily impact the other either positively or negatively.

For example, in the past, I might have thought I could have tensions in my marriage yet have no overflow into my vocation and that they were mutually exclusive. I believed that no one part of my life necessitated bleeding into another.

What a delusional mindset. One problem is that it minimizes the urgency of repentance in my marriage because, after all, other areas are "just fine." And so I can spend more hours working or keeping myself distracted with other pursuits (and often good pursuits) in the hope that things will just fix themselves in my marriage.

The problem is that *nothing* ever fixes itself when it comes to marriage. And contrary to whoever said it, time does *not* heal all wounds.

As men, we are fixers. We see a problem, assess it, and then get after it. See. Assess. Fix. Seems like a good way to live life. But how are you supposed to fix a broken marriage? If you are like me, I have viewed poor aspects of my marriage and froze as I could see no viable solution. I could easily see solutions to other people's marital issues, but I had no clue how to fix mine.

Ever been there?

I have—too many times. We then look for any excuse to unpack our heavy burdens and find somewhere else to place them. How many times I have unloaded the blame in our marriage onto my wife. And I do not even tell her. I just have mental conversations *with myself* about why the issue is not mine.

God allows me to sit in my own mess, if you will, and reap the mental stress and tension of going my own way. I begin to believe the delusion that I can simply pick off the bad fruit and be done with it. What I cannot see cannot hurt me. Or so I think.

But the root issue I must confront is not my sinful fruit. My root issue is a messed-up view of God and, hence, the reason I must daily recalibrate my view of him. I must combat the mentality that the words of the gospel are designed to show me where I need to give more effort. Rather, they are meant for me to come to the conclusion that what is asked is impossible. Yes, we are to strive in our Christian walk, but the essence of the gospel is about Jesus living *through* me and not just helping me when in trouble. It is easy for me to come to the wrong conclusion that if lust is robbing my life of marital joy, then quit lusting. If my sinful anger is shutting down my wife, then stop getting angry. If disengaging from my wife is leaving her embittered and angry, then start engaging. Just. Do. Better. I find this insidious attitude within me as well as other guys. It is not only a poor approach, but it is a sinful one. The *gospel* shapes the fruit in my life and provides the foundation to respond rightly even when my wife may not. *This* is when the gospel is active and alive within me.

"Shouldn't I try harder?" you might ask? In a word, "No." Because the truth of the matter is that your efforts are not what is going to change you or your marriage. To say it bluntly, my marriage is dysfunctional at times because my view of God is dysfunctional. *That* is my problem, and it is yours as well. You cannot claim to have a proper view of God while at the same time *not* pursue your wife. Your poor view of God is causing the disastrous fruit in your broken relationship with your wife.

But allow me to also add that my saying "you shouldn't try harder" is not a call to spiritual laziness. As husbands, we want to run *hard* in the *right* direction. If you watched the 2004 Winter Olympics, you might recall Matthew Emmons, an American rifle shooter. Emmons was competing in the three-position event, shooting from his stomach, knees, and feet. He was taking his final shot and had the lead. In firing, he miscalculated and fired at the wrong target one lane over. He finished in eighth place.

Effort does not matter if you are aiming at the wrong target. As men we just need to start running and in the right direction. It will be hard, and it will take discipline. That is why Paul reminds us in Philippians 2:12 to "work out your own salvation with fear and trembling."

Some years ago I listened to a message by C. J. Mahaney titled "The One to Whom I Will Look." It was absolutely impacting, and I listened to it again and again and again. His text was from Isaiah 66:1–2, and it says this about God:

> *Thus says the LORD: Heaven is my throne, and the earth is my footstool; what is the house that you would build for me, and what is the place of my rest? All these things my hand has made, and so all these things came to be, declares the LORD. But this is the one to whom I will look: he who is humble and contrite in spirit and trembles at my word.*

I have since memorized verse two, have repeated it often to myself, and have shared it with countless guys. God is omni-aware. There is certainly nothing that escapes his notice. He sees *all* people in *all* of time. Yet God says he takes special note of a person with specific characteristics: the one who is humble, contrite in spirit, and trembles at his word.

If you study the phrase in verse 2 "this is the one to whom I will look," it has the idea that God regards, pays attention to, or considers certain characteristics of people. It means he observes with favor, pleasure, or care those who model these specific attributes or qualities.[2]

So why these three? Why doesn't God say that he takes special interest in those who try harder, do better, and pick themselves up by their bootstraps? Because this trifecta in verse two is the irreducible minimum in what it takes to see my God accurately. In other words, humility, contriteness, and holy fear create the heart posture to properly view God, bring glory to him, and have joy in my life. Take away any one, and it all falls apart.

But please understand that humility, contriteness, and fearing God's Word are not prizes of self-effort. God will never ask you to be "more" of any of these three. Rather, they are the fruit of an active and redemptive gospel in my life that transforms my heart posture and sets its gaze on Jesus. God takes note of his working in my affections and desires and my responding to them.

So, let's unpack each of these.

GOD NOTICES HUMILITY

Why is humility listed first? And what is it about humility that so catches God's attention? Andrew Murray, a missionary to South Africa, has a good word for us about the importance of humility:

> *Humility is the only soil in which the graces root; the lack of humility is the sufficient explanation of every defect and failure. Humility is not so much a grace or virtue along with others; it is the root of all, because it alone takes the right attitude before God, and allows Him as God to do all.*[3]

Did you catch that? Humility *alone* takes the right attitude before God. It is *the* soil in which all other fruit grows. And that is not all. The late New Testament scholar John Stott adds to this view of humility:

> *At every stage of our Christian development and in every sphere of our Christian discipleship, pride is the greatest enemy and humility our greatest friend ... Pride is more than the first of the seven deadly sins; it is itself the essence of all sin.*[4]

Pride is my greatest enemy and humility my greatest friend.
Pride is itself the essence of all my sin.

Pretty weighty words. And a very honest narrative as to why my marriage is dysfunctional and sinful at times. Our western mindset has foolishly led me to believe that my leadership in my home is premised on two things: strength and being right. First, that for my wife to respect me and view me rightly, I must show courage and fortitude at all times. No chinks in this armor! And second, that being a leader means always being correct in my statements and assessments. Don't question me!

Pride is itself the essence of all my sin.

For me to biblically pursue my wife, it is going to necessitate that I not only view God correctly but also view myself as God sees me. And God says that he takes note of the one who is humble. That word means to be poor, needy, and weak. It is not just *saying* these words about myself but actually acknowledging that they are *true* about *me*.

Do I see myself as weak and in desperate need of God? Is my spiritual condition poverty stricken unless God intervenes in my life? Am I living a life of dependency because I know my own heart and its brokenness?

This is the first step to seeing God *and your marriage* rightly. And I have had God pull back the "curtains of my life" and expose my lack of humility and how it was failing my wife.

Let me provide you with a vivid example.

My dad was extremely involved in my life growing up, and I have no doubt that he loved me and loved Jesus. He did not grow up in a Christian home but, becoming a believer in the gospel early in his marriage, wanted to ensure that I had many of the spiritual blessings that he had not. We did a lot of father-son activities, and he talked much about the Christian life. But over the years, I noticed this "thread" showing up in our relationship. What do I mean? My dad was assertive and had a strong personality, and I had people-pleasing tendencies. To have one person who can come across as demanding relate with a person who likes to make sure everyone views him favorably is not a great combo package for a relationship. And it was this "thread" that began to weave itself tightly into many aspects of our relationship.

It was not long before this bled into my marriage. Don't get me wrong—my dad and I had many great times together. No other man shaped my heart like him. No other person invested in me like him. We were best of friends when I was growing up. But as Jerry Bridges has described the term "respectable sin," I managed my life to keep my sin hidden or to make it look less ugly than it was. What do I mean by "respectable sin"? It is any brokenness that I minimize because either it has become the norm in my life or I do not view it as seriously as *other* sins.[5]

Once I got married, my wife began to notice this dynamic as sin never infects just a person. Like a pebble dropped in a pool of water, the ripple effects carry out far and wide.

After a visit with my parents, who lived in a different state, my wife would approach me about this dynamic she saw in me and my dad. I heard her out, but I never really saw things from a biblical perspective. I was quick to offer up excuses for why things were not what they seemed, or I just internalized emotions. My pride blinded me again and again and again. The results were that I was more protective of keeping things in harmony with my dad than protecting my relationship with my wife. I devalued her opinions because she did not understand the full context. I minimized her pain and made excuses for my actions.

And as time went on and situations would periodically flare up between me and my dad, I found it easier to smooth things over with my wife than to biblically deal with my own sin and this relationship "thread" between a father and son. My "peace at all costs" mantra meant I was ignoring the Holy Spirit and pushing my wife into a corner.

Pride is my greatest enemy and humility my greatest friend.

But as my lens got skewed through which I viewed life, dealing with conflict became my greatest enemy and maintaining peace at any cost became my greatest friend. And this went on for the first fifteen to twenty years of my marriage. My lack of humility was both *affecting* and *infecting* my marriage.

And then one day God mercifully drew back the veil that had been covering my spiritual eyes. My wife and I were having this discussion about my dad and me, and once again I was driving my point home. And then she made a most impactful statement. I do not recall the exact words, though they were pointed, but I do remember her attitude of grace and spirit of love. And like an arrow leaving a bow and heading straight for the bullseye, this verbal arrow found its mark.

God used my wife's words that night in a powerful way—so powerfully that I was left speechless. I had nothing to say in response and no convincing arguments. God, in his mercy, opened my spiritual eyes and, for the first time, showed me *me*. And it was ugly. I saw my pride as God would have me see it. In my brokenness I confessed and repented of my people pleasing and pride toward my God and toward my wife.

And that began a new process of growth for me. And it began a renewed season of my marriage with my wife. And I was so grateful. The gift of repentance is not something to take lightly.

Humility is the only soil in which the graces root.

For my dad and me, though, things would get worse before they got better. And we ended up not speaking to each other for a period of months. But as a grace-giving and reconciliation-seeking God does, He was working on me while separately working on my dad. And when the soil of our hearts was ready, God reconciled us as father and son and allowed us to have a renewed relationship for a few years before God took him home. The gospel is greater. God notices humility.

GOD NOTICES A CONTRITE SPIRIT

In addition to a heart of humility, Isaiah also declares that God looks on the man who is contrite in spirit. "Contrite" is not a word we use much anymore, but it is rich in its meaning and implications. The dictionary definition is "caused by or showing sincere remorse; filled with a sense of guilt and the desire for atonement; penitent." The biblical definition of the word means "to be stricken or smitten." In its essence, to be contrite means that I see my sin as God sees it and, therefore, am quick to repent. I see my sin, I am stricken, and I repent and turn around.

This particular Hebrew word is used only two other times outside the book of Isaiah. It is also employed in 2 Samuel chapters 4 and 9 when speaking about Mephibosheth, who was the son of Jonathan and the grandson of King Saul.

Saul and Jonathan were killed at Mount Gilboa in a battle with the Philistines when Mephibosheth was only five years old. As was customary, the family of the king would also be killed by the enemy so that there would be no future lineage. To protect the future king, Mephibosheth's nurse picked him up and fled the premises. In her haste, Mephibosheth fell out of her arms, injured his feet, and became crippled. The word used for "contrite" is the very same word describing the condition of Mephibosheth: stricken or lame.[6]

When you read how this Hebrew word is used outside Isaiah, it presents a powerful mental image of what it means to be contrite. I see my sin, and I am stricken or smitten by my broken relationship with my wife and with Christ. No running. No excuses. And seeing my condition versus my righteous standing before God as a son brings me to repentance.

Not only does God take special note of those who model humility, but God also notices those who quickly admit their condition when shown the truth about their lives. And what does it look like when we are not contrite? We defend our character, our position, or our actions. We position ourselves to make us look favorable.

In the example I gave earlier about my dad, I was quick to defend to my wife the motives of my heart. This is a relational marriage killer, my friends. It is where we get the term "blind spot." Like driving a car and failing to see the vehicle to my left in my side mirror, I am blinded when the priority of my heart is *me*.

I love seeing me favorably!

But guys, take it from me. If you are a believer in the gospel of Jesus, God *will* kick your butt and allow you to taste the gravel of going your own way. And God does not do this because he is a mean overlord. He does it to bring you to the gift of repentance and to cultivate much fruit in your life. And of highest priority, he does it to bring him much glory. We must see our own lameness, like Mephibosheth, and fully grasp the condition of going the way of *our* own choosing.

Here is the strange thing: in an effort to defend myself with my wife in my actions with my dad, she and I both knew something was not right. I just did not want to face it because, if I did, it meant I would have to deal with my own rebel heart. And the truth was that I had absolutely no clue how to fix the relationship with my dad so I fell into self-preservation mode.

This turns out to be a critical part of the story because it dramatically illustrates how my poor view of God tainted my view of repentance. You see, I fell into the trap of thinking that my being right was what was going to bring me the most joy in my life. That positioning myself favorably was surely going to give me satisfaction.

But it didn't. In fact, my lack of a contrite spirit put a wedge between my wife and me. My poor view of God led me to a poor view of marriage. And I realized this on the night my wife gently and lovingly confronted me with her penetrating words. God began to break me and allowed me to truthfully see myself and then allowed me to more fully see him. And in that I saw the wonderful gift of repentance.

King David understood this well. Remember the story about David's sordid affair with Bathsheba and the prophet Nathan confronting him? Listen to David's words to God in Psalm 51: "For you will not delight in sacrifice, or I would give it; you will not be pleased with a burnt offering. The sacrifices of God are a broken spirit; a broken and contrite heart, O God, you will not despise" (verses 16–17).

Read it again. *A broken and contrite heart, O God, you will not despise.* God will not reject or disdain a heart of repentance before him. Why? Because repentance brings God much glory as he is calling a rebel heart toward him. Being contrite is not a head-hung-low-kicking-the-can-down-the-street type of spirit. Contriteness is an attitude that counters my sin and brokenness with an absolute confidence and dependence on God because *He is my satisfaction.* God values the humility of a contrite heart, but more importantly, God is about his glory.

To repent means to turn around. I was walking one way, but now I am walking the opposite direction. And when God opened my eyes that night in the conversation with my wife, he released all the fear and dread within me and overflowed me with his forgiveness and his grace. You see, I had forgotten that God is more about my joy than I am.

GOD NOTICES TREMBLING AT HIS WORD

I recall an epic trip some years ago that I made with my oldest daughter. We are serious North Carolina Tar Heel basketball fans, and I surprised her one birthday by taking her to a game on the campus of the University of North Carolina.

This was a bucket list item for sure.

One of the memories of the night was watching my daughter as we entered *the* Dean Smith Center. As we went through the ticket counter, we entered at the top of the arena, with memorabilia flooding our eyes. Wall posters of former and current players, championships won, and timelines of UNC history in basketball.

It was all there.

We were truly overwhelmed. After all of the games at the Smith Center we had only *viewed* on television, we were now *here*.

One of my favorite moments of the night was when her eyes caught one of the openings leading down to the basketball court. Eyes wide, shouting, "Dad … Dad … Dad, that's it! It's where they play! This is it!"

That made my night. All of her senses were honed in to that moment. There was an awe, this taking-it-all-in-nothing-else-matters type of response, a reverence of sorts for where we were actually standing.

This is, in a very small sense, what I think of when I ponder the final characteristic that God says is divinely attractive to him: trembling at his Word. In Isaiah 66:1–2, God does not issue a command, but rather he pulls us in close to reveal his own heart. What does God view with favor? What is attractive to him that he regards with special attention?

The first is having a humble spirit. The second is being quick to repent. The third? A reverential fear of God's Word. So, what is it about the way we interact with the Scriptures that gets God's attention?

ENGAGING IT FOR THE RIGHT PURPOSE

I believe God is pleased when I engage his word for the *right reasons*. And that means that I am always looking for Jesus no matter where I am reading in the Bible. It all points to him. In fact, without the gospel, there is no Word. "For all the promises of God find their Yes in him. That is why it is through him that we utter our Amen to God for his glory" (2 Corinthians 1:20).

Reading a passage of Scripture to "get my devotions done" does not cause God to take notice. But when I am reading the Bible with the intent to see Jesus so that I understand more of who he is and how I am to be more like him in loving my wife, I am reading with a heart motive that catches God's attention.

In addition, to read God's Word for the right purpose also means that I am seeing it as my source of spiritual life and direction and that it pertains not only to reading *about* Jesus but also looking *like* Jesus. Psalm 119:9–16 gives some insights into how David viewed God's words,

> *How can a young man keep his way pure?*
>   *By guarding it according to your word.*
> *With my whole heart I seek you;*
>   *let me not wander from your commandments!*
> *I have stored up your word in my heart,*
>   *that I might not sin against you.*
> *Blessed are you, O LORD;*
>   *teach me your statutes!*
> *With my lips I declare*
>   *all the rules of your mouth.*
> *In the way of your testimonies I delight*
>   *as much as in all riches.*
> *I will meditate on your precepts*
>   *and fix my eyes on your ways.*
> *I will delight in your statutes;*
>   *I will not forget your word.*

I have memorized this passage and quoted it to myself more times than I can recall because it displays the attitude that I desire to have toward God's revealed words to me. You come away with a sense that David revered God's truth and that it was paramount in his life.

It led him. It shaped his thoughts, affections, and desires. It held immeasurable value.

ENGAGING IT BECAUSE THERE IS NO GOSPEL WITHOUT IT

In recent years, I have come to more fully believe that it is *all about the gospel.* The gospel is much more than just about my salvation. It intersects every facet of my life.

We have to exercise caution when we use the word "gospel" so that it does not become a "junk-drawer" term, used so often in such general ways that it loses its meaning. But if I am truly all about the gospel, then one of the primary ways God speaks into my life is through his revealed Word, the Scriptures.

I encounter too many guys who give verbal assent that they need to be regularly encountering God through his Word yet simply are not reading it. Sure, there are countless excuses for why it does not happen, but God's truth is just not being read with any regularity.

"I don't have time." Right. Read.

"I don't understand everything." Got it. Read.

"I am not sure how to apply Scripture to my life." Okay. Read.

We cannot complain about our stale relationship with our wives and yet take no time to understand how God desires us to relate to them. It is all there—each of the sixty-six books weaves *a* story into *the* story about Jesus. Kevin DeYoung provides helpful perspective:

> *Apart from the Spirit working through Scripture, God does not promise to use any other means to guide us, nor should we expect him to. We have no promise in Scripture that God will speak to us apart from the Spirit speaking through His Word.*[7]

I would challenge you to cry out to God and ask him to change your desires and affections toward him and what he has written. Plead with him to put a love for his Word into your heart and stir up a heart of passion for his revealed truth. I cannot motivate my own self. I cannot try harder or do better. He must do the work.

I am afraid we have become such an experience-saturated culture that we look for too many encounters with God outside of what he has already declared. "The sum of your word is truth," David reflected in Psalm 119:160, "and every one of your righteous rules endures forever." All I need for life and godliness is found there, including how to genuinely love my wife in a manner that reflects Jesus loving his bride.

ENGAGING IT AS MY AUTHORITY

When my daughter and I visited the Smith Center, the surroundings held my daughter's complete focus. She was trembling with excitement because we *identify* with the North Carolina Tar Heels. They are a basketball *authority* for us.

On a much grander scale, the Bible is my authority for my marriage as well as my life. And as I have consistently read truth each day, God has taken it and intersected his Spirit with my spirit. In a word … transformation. And if the Scriptures are the governing rule for my life then it means by implication that I am not. It means choosing to not defend myself *in my moment* of frustration. It means choosing to engage my wife *in my moment* of passivity.

To view God's words with authority speaks to the very meaning of "trembles at my word" as found in Isaiah 66. It is a reverential fear of the words God has spoken that demand they be obeyed.

There are two primary reasons for us as men to have a holy awe toward the words God has spoken. The first is because of the authorship of these words: God Almighty. Listen to Isaiah's description of his awe of this majestic God:

> *In the year that King Uzziah died I saw the Lord sitting upon a throne, high and lifted up; and the train of his robe filled the temple. Above him stood the seraphim. Each had six wings: with two he covered his face, and with two he covered his feet, and with two he flew. And one called to another and said: "Holy, holy, holy is the LORD of hosts; the whole earth is full of his glory!" And the foundations of the thresholds shook at the voice of him who called, and the house was filled with smoke. And I said: "Woe is me! For I am lost; for I am a man of unclean lips, and I dwell in the midst of a people of unclean lips; for my eyes have seen the King, the LORD of hosts!" (Isaiah 6:1–5).*

The main reason I do not love and pursue my wife like Jesus pursues his church is because I view God as inconsequential, small, and distant. I have a poor view of an all-powerful God. And in viewing God as small, I end up regarding his words to me with apathy. Going back to my example with my dad and my wife, I was so caught up in managing the situation and maintaining peace at all costs that God's words to me became a distant voice. *I did not tremble at his words.* My pain and frustration spoke more loudly to me than the truth of my God.

Take heed, guys! This is what happens when we begin to set aside the principles God has already laid down for us in Scripture. *We* become our own authority, and when that happens, pursuing our wives takes on our own definition instead of the actual definition as modeled by Jesus.

The second reason to have a holy awe for the words God has spoken is due to the searching nature of Scripture. It exposes the very heart motives that we often cannot even see ourselves. Like a bright light that uncovers the hidden corners of a room, the Word of God reveals all things about my heart—motives, desires, and intents. "For the word of God is living and active, sharper than any two-edged sword, piercing to the division of soul and of spirit, of joints and of marrow, and discerning the thoughts and intentions of the heart" (Hebrews 4:12).

But you may say as a husband, "I'm not sure I want my thoughts and intentions revealed!" You actually do. And I do as well. David of the Old Testament clearly explains this toward the end of Psalm 139:23 when he says, "Search me, O God, and know my heart! Try me and know my thoughts! And see if there be any grievous way in me, and lead me in the way everlasting!"

What a model to us as husbands. David *asked* God to examine him thoroughly. He also asked God to know both his heart and his thoughts. The Hebrew word for "know" is "yada," which goes way beyond having an awareness of something. "Yada" means to have an experiential knowledge of someone or something through an up-close and personal connection.[8] God has interacted with David and is fully acquainted with him. And one more thing: David also asked God to uncover any grievous way within him. What David literally asked was for God to uncover any idols of his heart.

There is something about those words that almost wants to make me cringe as a husband. I am not sure I want to be understood by God in this way. But notice the equal sign that David communicates:

Intimate searching by God = Path of true freedom and joy

When God searched my own heart and exposed my fear of conflict over fearing him, when God revealed my pursuit of what made me comfortable over sacrificially loving my wife, when God used my wife to uncover my own blindness, the end result was freedom and joy. God does not use his Word to shame his children into obedience. Rather, it is employed to put me in an infinitely better place.

And my own blindness had caused me to forget.

But God. Oh, how many times I have appreciated those two words at the end of my sin. His words, as the Psalmist declares, are both a lamp to my feet and a light to my path. The searching power of the Scriptures through the Holy Spirit does indeed create an awe within me. For these words do surgery on my heart through the Holy Spirit. *They set me free from me!*

And oh, the freedom that I found and how that newfound freedom began a chain of events in my marriage for which I am ever grateful. When God began to form humility, a heart to repent, and a fear for his Word within me, it was at that point that God showcased his mercy in the heart of my marriage.

And not only did God begin to heal our relationship, but he gave us back lost years and grew our marriage to new levels of intimacy. Our fear of coming clean will often paralyze us as husbands. But let me say with assurance that it was the catalyst for some very unexpected and joyful results. I never knew that marriage could be *this good.*

So here is what you should be asking …

COMMUNION WITH GOD: Humble. Quick to repent. Tremble at God's Word. Why is your view of God in each of these areas so closely tied to how you view your wife?

COMMUNICATION WITH YOUR WIFE: Read Isaiah 66:1–2 to your wife. Ask her how each of these qualities could strengthen *your* leadership within your marriage.

COMMUNITY WITH OTHER MEN: Who or what has God used in your lives to challenge you in the areas of humility, quickness to repent, and trembling at his Word?

CHAPTER 3

WHEN MY IDENTITY DERAILS ME

Guys, let's face it. Our identities are often more fragile than we would care to admit. We work so hard to shape the perceptions of others, and yet it takes very little to shake our foundations. Our western culture has made it very clear that our performance drives our value. In other words, "doing" makes for "being."

And we feel this pressure as men.

What do I mean when I use the term "identity"? Simply stated, identity is what defines or characterizes us. It is where we find our significance, worth, or value as men. And where can we find our identity? Take your pick: hobbies, vocation, parenting, or marriage, to name a few.

Let's take a brief quiz. I am going to give you a name, and you tell me who they are. Ready?

Tom Brady.

Tom Hanks.

Donald Trump.

Steven King.

Were your answers "football player," "actor," "president," and "writer"? I am fairly certain they were. I asked you to tell me who they are, and I am guessing, for the vast majority of you, you provided an answer about what they do. And why? Because for each of these individuals, their performance has defined them or given them value. Each has crafted an identity because of what they do, at least to the public eye. To show you how much this mindset has permeated our culture, let's answer one more question.

Who is Michael Jordan? Whether you know basketball or not, your answer is probably close to "phenomenal basketball player." Yet what is interesting is that Michael's last year of playing professional basketball was in 2003.

THE FALSE IDENTITY OF PERFORMANCE

The problem with the mindset of identity equals performance is that it has thrown the biblical model of who we are on its head, and it is just one more manifestation of our brokenness in this world. "How so?" you may ask. "Isn't that who they are?" I could have picked any of a number of famous individuals. My point was simply to illustrate how easily we allow our identity to be shaped and nurtured by the things we do.

Why is this so critically important for us as men? It could be because marriage is not an easy relationship to flourish let alone maintain. It feels clunky at times, and if we were honest, it is easier to foster the relationships with the guys around us than it is our own wife. Love my wife as Jesus loves his church? What does that even *mean?*

Identity found in performance becomes a poor mistress. Yet we are tempted by it far too easily. And when loving our wives becomes too hard or feels too complex, the answer to "who am I?" takes on a myriad of answers.

Hunter.

Athlete.

Worker.

[Name the team] fan.

As guys, we are wired by God to subdue the earth, to lead, to manage. And it is a good thing—it really is. We love seeing things accomplished or an idea moved from thought to something tangible. We enjoy the hunt, building things, and exhausting physical triumphs. We delight in moving relationships or processes forward. We love to conquer. These are gifts of a good God. But if we are not cautious, it is not too long before these accomplishments become more than just the fruit of our efforts: they begin to define us. They morph from being satisfying to ultimately defining our satisfaction.

When I was a young parent, how my kids behaved or how they acted out to others was important to me. Right performance equaled a right heart. Their performing well, doing what they were told, saying "thank you," and modeling Christian behavior became the guidepost to which I measured not only how they were doing, but, more importantly, how I was doing. I wanted to be a "good father," and my kids' performance became an easy measuring stick for me.

And I will tell you firsthand, God allowed me to go after that hook and run the line out into the open water. I have three children, and I began looking for specific performance markers of what spiritual children should look like. When they were manifested, it gave me security that I was being the "good dad." But when they were not exhibited, I began to feel tension, and it shook my parental foundation. You see, my parenting became my identity and a security for who I was. And when things did not go according to *my plans* with my kids, I ramped up the efforts to bring my world back into equilibrium.

And it very nearly derailed our relationships, especially with my son. "But God." How many times have I used that phrase in describing God's rescuing process with my rebel heart. God did intervene, crushing me with his grace, to return me to a better joy and satisfaction. The Holy Spirit unveiled to me that my identity was being found in the performance of another—my kids—and that my endeavors to manage my kids' behavior were only pushing them away from me. God has a strong term for our misplaced identity problems: idolatry. And in receiving God's discipline, he changed the affections of my heart and opened my spiritual eyes. Today, I have amazing relationships with my kids, and I am frequently reminded of how God performed a rescue mission in my life.

My inner tension and angst were the telltale signs that parenting had become a false identity for me. It had become my idol, and, in doing so, it created a disappointing identity for myself. I was looking to "right-hearted children" as to what gave me worth or value. And when the relationships started moving away from my plan, I felt overwhelmed as things seemed out of control—or out of my control, I should say.

A HUSBAND'S TRUE AND BETTER IDENTITY IN KING JESUS

If you are a believer in the gospel, if you have submitted to Jesus as sovereign King in your life, if you are trusting only in the finished work of Jesus Christ to save your rebel heart and give you new life, then you now have a new identity. And when we choose to replace *this* identity with one of our own choosing, disastrous and disappointing effects will overwhelm us.

The apostle Peter puts this reality in beautiful language for us:

> *But you are a chosen race, a royal priesthood, a holy nation, a people for his own possession, that you may proclaim the excellencies of him who called you out of darkness into his marvelous light. Once you were not a people, but now you are God's people; once you had not received mercy, but now you have received mercy (1 Peter 2:9–10).*

I am a son of God today because God chose me for the purpose of bringing him glory. His mercy reached out to me, and now I am one of God's people.

> *Blessed be the God and Father of our Lord Jesus Christ, who has blessed us in Christ with every spiritual blessing in the heavenly places, even as he chose us in him before the foundation of the world, that we should be holy and blameless before him. In love he predestined us for adoption to himself as sons through Jesus Christ, according to the purpose of his will, to the praise of his glorious grace, with which he has blessed us in the Beloved (Ephesians 1:3–6).*

Misunderstanding this gospel reality will tempt us away from our identity in Jesus and into a self-identity of our own making. This identity built on self turns out nothing like how we had hoped the story would end. Salvation in Jesus is the great exchange: my life for his. John Piper brings clarity to this when he states:

> *Christian selfhood is not defined in terms of who we are in and of ourselves. It's defined in terms of what God does to us and the relationship he creates with*

*us and the destiny he appoints for us. God made us who we are so we could make
known who he is. Our identity is for the sake of making known his identity.*[1]

So, you might be asking what all this identity stuff has to do with you as a
husband. In a word, "everything." From my own experiences, I would say my
own failings and frustrations as a man in loving my wife have had identity issues
at their root. The reason for this is that we have been led to believe our success in
marriage is found in the same ideals we use for any other challenge. Let me ask you
a question: if you run up against an enormous challenge that is staring you in the
face, how do you resolve it? Yes, the Christian answer may be to "trust in God," but
I find I am more often inclined to live out the mantra that seems most natural for
us as men: try harder, give more effort, focus more attention, and just do better.

Performance.

Guess what happens when you encounter an enormous challenge in your
marriage? What do you do when a rocky, tumultuous, or stale relationship with
your wife has become the norm? You end up using the same tools from the same
tool belt: try harder, give more effort, focus more attention, and just do better.

So, let me ask you, how is that going for you? Seeing great results? Or seeing
the same results as before? My guess is your answer is the latter. This mindset is
neither effective in pursuing your wife nor pleasing to God. What it will do is
plant thoughts in your mind that end up looking like these:

"I keep trying to love my wife, and all it seems to do is make things worse."

"I try to pursue her, but she never responds to it."

"I am such a failure as a husband. No matter what I do, we just argue."

"Things go okay for a while, but then it always goes back to what it was."

If your marriage is in decline, my guess is that you have had one or more of
these thoughts. At times, marriage seems too hard, too complex, and too much
work. And hearts drift. And you stop caring.

A FULLER PICTURE THAT CREATES PURPOSE

Can I offer you another way? A path that has not only worked for me but
also has brought intense joy into my marriage? It all began with recalibrating

my identity. My guess is that you are familiar with the marital roles presented in Ephesians 5 for a husband and wife: love and respect. A husband is to love his wife; a wife is to respect and honor her husband. We do God's Word a great disservice when we view these as simply two commands in isolation. Ephesians 5:22 and 25 are very clear in their intent: "Wives, submit to your own husbands, as to the Lord." And "Husbands, love your wives, as Christ loved the church and gave himself up for her."

Without understanding the larger context, we go away with our instructions of what we need to do: love our wives like Jesus would love them. But that picture is incomplete. There is a fuller picture with a grander scheme and a clearer identity. It is this:

For a husband: God loves his Son. Jesus loves his church. A husband loves his wife.

For a wife: Jesus submits to his Father. The church submits to Jesus. A wife submits to her husband.

Though this is a book written for men and about men, there must be the inclusion of the wife's role to appreciate this full identity. My identity as a husband is now in something other than me and my performance. It looks to the performance of another. Scripture is clear that God is well pleased with his Son (Matthew 17:5; Mark 1:11) and that Jesus loves his bride the church (Ephesians 5:25; 1 John 4:10; John 10:10). *Those* are the examples that precede loving my wife. And realize that these go beyond mere examples. They are the very source by which I am called to love my wife. But the truth of the matter is loving my wife like God loves his Son and Jesus loves his church are impossibilities for me *unless* I have the identity to which I am called as a son.

If you read through John chapters 15 and 16, you begin to see a theme about the Trinity and how God the Father, Son, and Holy Spirit work in concert with each other for the benefit of adopted sons and daughters.

God the Father is introduced in this grand metaphor as the Vinedresser. He tends to each of the branches with individual love and care (John 15:1–2). And his work is very intentional—maximum fruit. His shaping process includes cutting off shoots that fail to contribute to good growth, including "branches" of condemnation that cause us to live as fearful and shameful sons.[2]

Romans 8:28–29 has very clear verbiage about our identity:

> *And we know that for those who love God all things work together for good, for those who are called according to his purpose. For those whom he foreknew he also predestined to be conformed to the image of his Son, in order that he might be the firstborn among many brothers.*

God works all things for our good, and that good is to be conformed to, or made like, Jesus Christ. God is faithful in his agenda of making us look more like Jesus as Jesus is the perfect representation of the fruit of the Spirit (Galatians 5:22–23).

Next is Jesus. If his Father is the one who tends his fields with care, then Jesus is the living Vine to whom we our attached. He emphasized this very point by proclaiming "… for apart from me you can do nothing." The Greek word for "nothing" has no special nuance in Jesus's statement. It means "nothing." He did the work for me. He performed perfectly on my behalf. And the Father accepted his Son's obedience to make reparation for my hideous sin. Here is the great exchange: "For our sake he made him to be sin who knew no sin, so that in him we might become the righteousness of God" (2 Corinthians 5:21).

There is no "Jesus plus my self-efforts." And it is because of this very mindset that we make messes of our marriages. Jesus's righteousness now secures my righteousness, but as long as I try to add in "me" to the equation, I will end up discouraged and disillusioned when it comes to experiencing the joy of a marriage in full pursuit.

That does not mean we are not to strive after looking like our elder brother, Jesus. But if we are going to have the very same love with which Jesus loves us and have the very same joy with which Jesus has joy over us, then it will take being attached to the Vine to have our affections and desires radically changed to produce *his* fruit (John 15:8–11).

Finally, there is the Holy Spirit. The blessed Holy Spirit. My Comforter and Helper. But yet the oft-ignored member of the Trinity. John 16:7–14 speaks to how the Holy Spirit works in concert with the Father and Son and is essential to a correct identity. One of the roles of the Spirit is to convict. Convict the world of sin, convict the believer of righteousness, and convict the prince of this world of his already-accomplished defeat.

"Convict" also has the meaning to convince. It speaks of the office of a judge, who by receiving clear and compelling evidence, is able to shed light on a situation that was once clouded from truth.[3] In other words, the Spirit convinces believers of their righteous standing before God. Why? As men, we easily fall into condemnation of ourselves, especially as it relates to the health of our marriages. And the Spirit convinces us primarily through reading the Scriptures.

How do you relate to the following story? I blow it in my marriage, and there is a setback. Again. And, as a guy, I do not reach out to my community of men for perspective and prayer. I go solo and counsel myself. And my self-counseling usually leads me into despair. The Spirit then becomes essential because he indwells me. He is reminding me of my sonship and my righteous standing with God, that Jesus's love is the source of my love and that Jesus's joy is the source of my joy. *This* is my true and authentic identity. It is my calling.

My biggest struggle is not *what* I am called to but more the *how*. And what the *how* looks like is going to be dictated by *where* I am finding my identity. I clearly recall the frustration I was feeling in trying to love my wife in a way that looks like Jesus loving his church. The more I tried the worse I failed. I could feel the tension within me of trying to reconcile God's desires with my inabilities. I remember praying something to the effect of this: "God, I have no idea how to love this woman in the way that *she* needs, in the manner that *you* desire. I am having too many mental conversations with myself and falling into despair and anger. I find myself blaming her more often than not for the lack in our marriage. I give. I need you to do *something* because I cannot do *anything* to fix my mess."

This was a process by which God began to undo *my* identity and then place it in *his* identity. And do you know what happened? God began to change the very desires and affections of my heart for my wife. I cannot explain it. This was a monumental "Aha!" moment in my growth as a husband. It was the realization that I cannot change what my heart wants. I cannot just decide one day to biblically love my wife, to meet her needs, and to serve her well. Oh, I can put out more effort, but without the Trinity working in concert in my life, I was bound to a slavery of my own making.

It is the difference between trying to love my wife more versus a love that just overflows within me. It is the difference between doing for my wife versus serving her because she is always in my "crosshairs." I was desperate, and God initiated within me. The Father pruning me, the Son providing the life-giving power, and the Spirit always pointing to what is true about me *in Christ*. And in a culture that shouts, "Just be true to yourself," it has never been truer for me as a husband that being true to myself has only fooled me into trusting in a weak and frail identity: me.

Please do not gloss over this chapter. I would encourage you to reread it and ask God to search your heart and expose those rebel parts that are pushing the identity of Jesus to the side. Do you want a fulfilling I-can't-believe-things-could-be-this-good marriage? Do you want a marriage that pictures Jesus's love for his bride? Do you desire a marriage that pleases God? Because whether or not you realize it, this is what you covenanted to when you said "I do" on your wedding day. This is the grander picture to which you committed. I do not care what your vows did or did not include. This is how God views your relationship with your bride. He created marriage, so he has the right to make it picture what he desires for his glory and your joy. You cannot fake it. You cannot add your tiresome efforts or small thoughts into the process. It demands being all in. It demands a full surrender and a death to self. It demands a proper identity found in the One who has the power to change both your heart and your desires for your wife. And his name is Jesus.

So here is what you should be asking …

COMMUNION WITH GOD: How is understanding God's love for his Son and Jesus's love for his church a prerequisite to loving your wife?

COMMUNICATION WITH YOUR WIFE: Read Ephesians 1:3–6 to your wife. Explain why you as a husband must grasp the importance of your identity in Jesus to be able to love her well.

COMMUNITY WITH OTHER MEN: Why are we as guys so prone to associate identity with performance? How is Jesus the better identity in loving our wives?

CHAPTER 4

THE FOUR ESSENTIALS OF HUSBANDING

Have you ever heard these words before?

"Be the husband God created you to be."

"God wants you to be a spiritual leader in your home."

"Be a biblical man."

To which you may echo, "Yes! I want these for my own life!" But if you were asked to define what each of those statements mean or asked to describe what they look like in your life, things might come to a grinding halt.

Back in a "prior life" I had the privilege to teach at a Christian university. Among others, I taught a class for guys about what God desired for them as men. We had some amazing, eye-opening, and transparent discussions. And one of their assignments was to go into our surrounding cities and towns and ask men and women this question, "What does it mean to be a man?" There were almost as many varying answers as there were people being questioned. There were some common responses, but by and large, people had their own idea of what it meant to be a man. It was interesting to hear how their families or surrounding cultures shaped their views of manhood.

When my girls were younger, they loved to watch the Disney movie *Mulan*. If you have never watched this movie, it follows the story of a young Chinese girl named Mulan living in a patriarchal society. She is dismayed to hear that her ill and aging father has been drafted into the military, and so she impersonates a man to step in for him. In one of the more comical parts of the movie, she is seen training with her fellow recruits, and as Disney is known for, the characters burst into song. In this particular rendition, the strong and exemplary military leader, Captain Li Shang, is utterly frustrated with his sad lot of military men he has been assigned. He sternly looks at them and tells them he will make men out of them yet.

(Enter song with catchy chorus)

> *Be a man*
> *We must be swift as a coursing river*
> *Be a man*
> *With all the force of a great typhoon*
> *Be a man*
> *With all the strength of a raging fire*
> *Mysterious as the dark side of the moon*[1]

It's a fun song, and to this day, when my daughters are in the car with me, we still sing it with a gusto that would have made Captain Li Shang proud. But are these the defining aspects of manhood? Swiftness, force, strength, and a sense of mystery about us? You're right, there is not much in this song in terms of theology. But it serves to prove a point. Our culture throws us much as to what it means to be a man as well as a husband. But yet, if we are honest, it is challenging to get our minds around it and even know what it means. Everyone has their own ideas and preconceived notions about these topics. It seems easy to verbalize, but there is a serious disconnect between expressing words and living life. And so many guys, young and old, wander through this life with a vague sense of manhood or being a husband, chasing after a target that is fuzzy at best.

Without a clear and focused bullseye of godly manhood, the defining elements of being a man sink to ever-deepening levels. Harsh words. Violence. Apathy. Demanding our way. Idolatry. Isolation. Viewing women as objects. No pursuit of our bride. A poor leadership pandemic.

And this among those who claim Jesus as their Savior and King.

So where are we to turn?

I look at the state of us men today, and it becomes weighty at times. I listen to men talk about their lives, I hear their struggles, and I see their pain. I see young men without a compass guiding their lives and a lack of older guys willing to come alongside. The generation gap seems to just be getting wider and the chasm deeper. I see guys doing one of two things: 1) either jumping the ship of faith, saying something to the effect that they are not sure about this stuff anymore, or 2) putting on the "everything is okay" mask and quietly disengaging from what is relevant.

Another one lost.

We've been lied to, guys. We have been so led down the path of "be your own person" or "be true to yourself" that many guys, regardless of the age, do not have a clear target in front of them on which to place their aim. Being true to myself could mean a different bullseye every day. And it appears that there are such gaps between age groups of men that guys are often left with only their peers, swimming in their own pool of ignorance.

We have been taught well to follow our own compass. The problem is that my own compass, heavily influenced by emotions and pressures around me, easily steers me into the rocky shoals of life where I end up shipwrecked.

I am very grateful, though, for the hope that arises because of Jesus. I love how Eric Mason puts it:

> *I think there's a crisis in manhood in our culture, and I believe Jesus is the answer to that. We need the gospel. We need it more than books. More than studies. More than groups. We need the life-giving, identity-establishing, purpose-defining gospel of Jesus Christ.*[2]

God has called us to be manly men. To be men who look like Jesus. But what does that mean? Do I do certain things? Do I act with certain behaviors? This quickly becomes a dangerous dead-end. For if I find my identity as a guy in my performance, what happens when those crutches in my life take a hit? You got it. As we saw in the prior chapter, I fall hard.

In our society today, it is easy to get hooked by the "do this, and you will get quick and massive results immediately" mindset. We all know *deep down* that nothing done quickly with minimal effort will yield heroic-type results. But we still chase after them.

I think our "rules for biblical manhood" can easily fall into this trap as well. There is no quick fix for being a spiritual and loving leader and husband to your wife. There just isn't. But I do believe there is great benefit in looking at common points of failure among men and countering those with a strategic and biblical plan. I have seen too many examples of men losing sight of the prize and simply fading out of the picture. It is almost like a spiritual paralysis—they do not know what to do and so they do … nothing. The problem is that "nothing" is a highly volatile state in which to exist.

Part of being a husband that brings glory to God and has immense joy in marriage is having the proper tools for your spiritual tool belt and knowing how to effectively use them. Some years ago, a book was recommended to me that totally reshaped my view of being a biblical man and husband. The name of the book is *Raising a Modern Day Knight*.[3] The primary emphasis of this well-written text is on the father-son relationship. Its theme is built on the intentional process of how a boy became a knight in medieval times. From that theme the author springboards to the intentional process of a boy becoming a man through adopting four biblical ideals. I have presented them to my own son, I have taught them to a number of guys on the college level, and I have laid them out for men in our church.

And so I would like to offer you these same four pillars as they provide a practical model for husbands as well. You need to understand that these are not silver bullets and that quoting these four ideals will not give you a better marriage. God must do the work of changing your heart and aligning your desires with his. But they are a helpful place to begin.

JESUS REJECTED PASSIVITY

Passivity takes many forms and can plague your life in every area, but I want to stay dialed in to your marriage and your relationship with your wife. As it concerns the relationship with your wife, being passive means to choose not to engage when you *could* engage. It is a lack of paying attention to your wife. You have no plans for her growth or nurturing. You allow your marriage to play out with no strategy or goals. Things just exist.

You might be passive if you think your marriage is going to somehow drift into being good. You might be passive if you hear the words of your wife but never desire to listen to the cares of her heart. You might be passive if you believe your wife is the chief of sinners.

I can sniff out passivity in a guy within five minutes. Why? Because it used to define my own marriage. As my own daughters have entered womanhood, I have spoken with them many times about red flags in a potential future husband. Being passive is right at the top of my list. My girls know this one well. In fact, we were having a conversation as a family about my writing this book. My youngest chimed in with her idea for a title. "Hey Dad," she said, "you should name your book *Conquering Passivity: A Marriage Handbook for Jack Wagons.*"

Brilliant.

When I was in the early years of my marriage, I did not like conflict, and I brought that attitude into my marriage. Passivity was a defining characteristic of how I chose to love and lead my wife. My wife, who is a strong personality and "git-r-done" type of woman, sensed this within me. She did not like it nor desire it. But it produced a response within her. She experienced the passivity. To her, it was my seeing her struggle and choosing not to step in. It did not matter the reason. I saw something going on and did not engage her at the heart level. Looking back, I believe it was a combination of two factors. First, I was somewhat fearful of what would result once I chose to dive into this situation. It was messy and complex. Second, I did not really know how to change things from their current state.

As a result, she became more independent in our marriage, and since I was not leading like Jesus, she took the lead within our home in areas that I should have been pursuing. In her words, she grew independent both mentally and emotionally. When we both said "I do" on our wedding day, two were to become one. But my passivity tempted her away from this one flesh relationship and drew her to be independent once again. She admits it was a sinful response on her part, but it was a defense mechanism. Roles began to reverse, and things got out of sync. I loved my family. I was present in a physical sense. But I was not viewing my wife through the eyes of how Jesus views his bride. He initiates. He engages us as his bride to make us holy. He has an agenda for us: to look like him. His affections are intentional and purposeful. He sees our messiness and willingly steps into it with us.

The Bible presents the best of contrasts when it comes to this topic of passivity. Adam versus Jesus. When Adam was created and placed in the garden of Eden, God was very specific about his role and the prohibition placed upon Adam: do not eat of the Tree of the Knowledge of Good and Evil.

Pretty clear.

And if you read Genesis 2, God and Adam had this conversation *before* Eve was created. He was to protect Eve by teaching her God's ways. From the very beginning, Adam was designed by God to protect his woman and be more concerned about her welfare than his own. It is interesting to note in Genesis 3 that when Satan the serpent craftily approached Eve, Adam was right there. When pleasure was calling out, the voice of God became a distant noise. When the serpent tempted her away, Adam's passivity left his bride in grave danger, and he did nothing about it. Adam did not protect the truth given by his Creator, and he did not protect his wife when she was in peril. He saw his wife struggling with her conclusions about God and chose to stand by.

And the consequences of Adam's response could not have been more severe for us as husbands. For the "first Adam," as our federal head, secured the rebel-heartedness of each of us as we do daily battle with our heart's inclination to be in awe of ourselves and lose our awe of God.

But Jesus ... but Jesus came as the *second* Adam, not just as a living being but rather as a *life-giving* spirit. He came to undo, fully and finally, the carnage left behind by the passive Adam. He obeyed the will of his Father and went as a lamb to the slaughter. And to what extent did he protect *his* bride? He *died* when I should have been *cursed.* He was crushed by his Father when it should have been me.

Jesus *initiated.* He countered the temptation to be passive by initiating with his bride because of his great love for her. When he saw his bride struggling in her sin, he initiated and went *to* her. Jesus knew it was going to be more than just uncomfortable to jump into our broken mess: he was going to be murdered. He saw his creation in rebellion and without hope, and he willingly engaged us at the heart level. Being passive is not just a personality type: it is a rebel-hearted sin that originated from our father Adam when he chose not to protect his beloved. It is an active and willful choice to *not* love our wives as Jesus loves his church. We need help. We need Jesus.

JESUS ACCEPTED RESPONSIBILITY

To accept responsibility as husbands translates to embracing the calling that God has given to us.

> *Husbands, love your wives, as Christ loved the church and gave himself up for her, that he might sanctify her, having cleansed her by the washing of water with the word, so that he might present the church to himself in splendor, without spot or wrinkle or any such thing, that she might be holy and without blemish (Ephesians 5:25–27).*

Does this overwhelm you when you read it? It does me. To engage my wife in such a manner that it produces holiness within her? To love her in a way that models the grace and kindness of her Father? To be part of her sanctification process as a daughter of King Jesus? It is a responsibility that is more far reaching than what I was thinking on the day I said "I do." It is a sacrificial type of service and devotion to my wife that draws from an inner strength and motivation that I do not have on my own. When I read these verses, there are thoughts of "That's *my* role?" Our culture, societal influences, as well as media have formed ideals about good husbanding: be faithful, show interest, provide for her, and do nice things every once in a while—you know, kind of the Hallmark movie theme. But these verses go far deeper. To fully embrace *this* sort of responsibility peels away the layers of my heart and gets down to its very motives and desires. There is no flipping of a heart switch from "off" to "on." There is no coming by this naturally. It takes the second Adam, Jesus, being a life-giving spirit to me.

Adam was given three responsibilities when he was placed in the garden of Eden: obey God's commands, tend to the garden, and protect his wife. They were his responsibilities, and they provided him purpose. The fulfilling of them would lead to great joy and satisfaction. But in a single moment of time, it all unraveled.

The serpent spoke lies to Eve, and Adam failed in all his responsibilities. Every last one. And when God confronted Adam about his disobedience, he did the exact opposite of accepting responsibility: he placed blame. "The woman whom you gave to be with me, she gave me fruit of the tree, and I ate" (Genesis 3:12).

When Adam was accused of disobedience, of which he was guilty, he was quick to point the blame at his bride. When Jesus, the second Adam, was accused of sin, of which he was innocent, he *protected* his bride. God the Father initiated a plan for the redemption of mankind, and Jesus joyfully and willingly accepted this responsibility and drank his Father's cup of wrath to the very last dregs.

I see too many guys today, including myself, who did not know what they were *really* signing up for when they got married. They failed to read the "small print" in their Bibles. They had their own notions as to what it meant to have the responsibility of loving and serving their wives. It *is* a weighty thing, and it gets heavier the older I get. And it becomes more burdensome as I watch other guys failing to accept their mantles.

I see more poor marriages than I desire to see. There are some that are transformed and succeed, and others that do not. And there seems to a common thread that can predict if the marriage will be transformed or not. It is this: will the husband accept responsibility for the state of his marriage, or will he push the blame to his wife?

Enter James. James has struggled with lust for most of his life. His marriage is a wreck, and he knows it. He does not pursue his wife neither is he part of her growth. He speaks harshly to her. He knows he has a very poor view of God and how God views him as a son. But yet when I speak to him, he is very quick to point out the faults of his wife and how she does this and doesn't do that. How can he take it anymore? Oh sure, he knows he has areas to grow, but it always comes across as if she is more broken. Her sin seems so much greater to James, so the responsibility lies with her to change.

I know about this firsthand in my own marriage. I think back to some earlier days of our marriage when our three kids were living in our home, and life was crazy busy. You know what I mean: there were music lessons to be attended, sporting events to be cheered, science projects to be rushed, rooms to be cleaned, doctor appointments to be kept, and relationships to be nurtured. And then we were fitting full-time jobs into the mix. I loved being a parent, but those seasons of life were extremely exhausting.

It was during one such season when I realized that intimacy for me and my wife was in a holding pattern. As kids got older they stayed up later. My wife and I finished a day and by bedtime were totally exhausted. I began to have these seed thoughts that perhaps my wife was just not interested in sexual intimacy anymore and that things were just getting stale. Instead of talking with her about this, I chose to have mental conversations with myself. And if you are like me, these conversations never ended up in a good place. I began shifting the blame for how things were to my wife and felt justified in doing so. My responsibility in all this seemed dim to the glaring faults of my wife. "Here I ... and she doesn't even. ..." "Why can't she ... ?" "Does she really think that ... ?"

This issue was compounded by the passivity I was displaying by not wanting to engage my wife because I was fearful of what she might say or what this conversation would turn into. So, one Saturday we went out to breakfast together, and I got the nerve up to discuss this. I had my "gospel gun" loaded to push back on any points she might make. I hesitantly and cautiously entered the conversation and began to lay out my concerns about our lack of sexual intimacy. She listened. And before I was even halfway through my finely-crafted defense, she said to me, "Then why don't you just pursue me?" I still recall that moment. Have you ever watched a movie where a character has some epiphany and the camera zooms up on his shocked face? That was me. It was as if all strategic thought froze. And I still had a few substantial points left!

Darn that woman!

"Why don't you just pursue me?" It was a fair question but not one I was ready to answer.

The bigger issue was not our love life. The bigger issue was that I was not accepting responsibility for the pursuit of my wife but rather shifting blame. And allow me to interject a quick thought: This is not saying my wife has no areas of needed growth in her spiritual life—she clearly sees her need of grace, but it is acknowledging our propensity as husbands to have blinders on when viewing our marriages. We too easily resist responsibility so that our brokenness does not look so broken to ourselves or to our wives.

Jesus did not accept his responsibility from his Father because "that's what guys do—we just grit it out." Rather, he embraced his calling because there was joy in the midst of it. This is critical to understand because it is too easy to miss in the midst of the mundaneness of marriage. Look at Jesus. "Looking to Jesus, the founder and perfecter of our faith, who for the joy that was set before him endured the cross, despising the shame, and is seated at the right hand of the throne of God" (Hebrews 12:2).

It is peaceful and effortless to accept our responsibility as husbands when the wind is at our backs and the sun is shining in our faces. And we should give thanks for those seasons of life. But there are times when the everyday of life can suck it right out of us. When that happens, I am tempted to move toward passivity and set aside the responsibility to pursue my wife and engage her. So, what do we do? John Piper helps us picture this rightly: "We fight sin by a sovereign joy that masters us and severs the root of all competing and controlling pleasures."[4]

There it is. We fight the urge to lay aside responsibilities with our wives because of the sovereign joy of Jesus Christ. But it is going to demand more than just resistance. It is also going to require a holy courage.

JESUS LED COURAGEOUSLY

Leading courageously is not just taking a path, but it is taking a path that others might not be so quick to jump on—a path to action. Resolving conflict biblically. Setting aside personal agendas. Having a difficult conversation. Stepping out in faith to allow God to stretch you, even though you know that it might be painful, even though you know it might cost you. I must pray for courage in my life because my flesh too often wants to take the path of least resistance—the path that is going to help me feel the least amount of tension. "Courage is almost a contradiction of terms," asserts G. K. Chesterton. "It means having a strong desire to live taking the form of a readiness to die."[5]

This is what we are called to in our marriages—"taking the form of a readiness to die." Once again we must note the comparison between the first Adam and the second Adam: Adam's temptation in the garden of Eden versus Jesus's in the wilderness. The temptations are similar, yet the outcomes could not be starker.

When the serpent enters the picture in Genesis 3:1–6, Adam was in a very innocent surrounding with no sin having corrupted God's creation. The garden was a paradise—a perfect environment for obedience. God took care of his prized creation. And yet in that paradise, as he listens to the serpent, we find Adam's flesh crying out for something more than having God: he wanted to *be* God and make his own choices, determining what was good and determining what was evil. God was no longer trustworthy. The temptation posed to Adam lasted the time it took for the conversation to happen. And in a moment of truth, Adam succumbed to his own feelings and took the fruit and initiated sin and death for every human being that would ever be born. God's judgment fell so directly on Adam because he heard the original command given by God and was accountable to teach it to his wife. "Adam was not deceived," 1 Timothy 2:14 reminds us, "but the woman was deceived and became a transgressor." Adam had abandoned his calling and had traded it for temporary pleasure.

In Matthew 4:1–11, the narrative describes another temptation, a temptation involving Jesus and Satan. Yet while some of the details might be comparable, the results are not. We are told early on in Matthew 4 that Jesus was not in a paradise like Adam but rather in the wilderness. "Then Jesus was led up by the Spirit into the wilderness to be tempted by the devil. And after fasting forty days and forty nights, he was hungry" (Matthew 4:1–2).

Jesus's conditions could not have been more different. Whereas Adam was in the very best of surroundings living in community with Eve, Jesus was in the wilderness, a lonely, desolate, solitary setting in which to suffer hardship. It was barren, not only of the sustenance of Eden, but also of the help and protection of others. This was a setting in complete contradiction to the setting of Adam. For forty days his defenses were worn down through exposure and hunger. For forty days Satan appealed to his emotions and passions to offer him "another glory," a glory outside the obedience of his Father.

Jesus exhibited great courage in fighting his foe. While his body and emotions were screaming for relief, Jesus displayed uncommon courage and trust in his Father to endure this season of temptation. He walked through it and felt the full brunt—every single step—but wrapped himself in the cloak of truth and grace and fought the glory being offered to him.

This is a call to us as men and as husbands. We are being offered every excuse to leave the fight. We are being sold every line that Jesus is simply *not* better. He is not better than our passivity, he is not better than our anger, he is not better than our lust, and he is not better than our pursuits of things other than our wives. Our poor view of Jesus has led us to be husbands who cower in the corners, forgetting we have a savior with which to identify.

> *For we do not have a high priest who is unable to sympathize with our weaknesses, but one who in every respect has been tempted as we are, yet without sin. Let us then with confidence draw near to the throne of grace, that we may receive mercy and find grace to help in time of need (Hebrews 4:15–16).*

We are told to approach this throne of grace with confidence. And that word "confidence" translates to "cheerful courage."[6] Yes, you read that correctly. We are commanded to approach our advocate with cheerful courage. Why? Because my elder brother Jesus has the mercy and grace I so desperately need to love and lead *my* bride in a manner that would remind her of Jesus loving *his* bride.

JESUS EXPECTED THE GREATER REWARD

If your marriage has plateaued or is in decline, it can be incredibly difficult to see a way forward, that things will ever be any different than they are today. I get it. I have been there. Part of the reason is that our efforts have never changed anything before, so why should they now? And part of the reason is that perhaps peace in our marriages has become the endgame rather than an ultimate satisfaction in Jesus.

Many of us have set the bar far too low in our marriages for what we view as "reward." As I reflect on my relationship with my wife, I see a number of objectives that have become my pursuit:

Being right.

Having the last word.

Feeling strong.

Getting my way.

All of these outcomes have enticed me and given me reason to think that they are going to be fulfilling, provide satisfaction, and lead to joy. The emphasis, though, on this final biblical ideal is on the phrase "greater reward." By giving my energies to false delights, I fail to recognize that I am eroding the foundation of my marriage.

We must expect the *greater* reward. This means that in the pressures of gratifying myself right now and for my cause, I make decisions that show Jesus is better. That in following Him, he is the true and superior reward. That there is a better sense, a more noble sense, a longer-lasting sense of joy when I yield in desperate surrender to a God who desires my joy more than I desire it for myself.

This is not easy to do as it demands decision-by-decision evaluation of thinking, and it demands a changed heart. When you look at the final days of Jesus, how was he able endure as he did and stay the course of his mission to the very end? It was the greater reward of joy. Let's look at Hebrews 12:2 once again: "Looking to Jesus, the founder and perfecter of our faith, who for the joy that was set before him endured the cross, despising the shame, and is seated at the right hand of the throne of God."

The greater reward for Jesus was found in glorifying his Father. What he endured, he endured for the sake of his bride and for the great love he had for her. In the mundane moments of our marriages, though, the shininess of cheap and worthless trinkets catches our eyes and distracts us. There have been many times in my marriage where, in a heated conversation, my primary objective was to posture myself to look favorable. In the midst of conflict, the grand narrative looks extremely small. I can feel its cravings within me. I can sense its pull as if it were physically accosting me. I want to be right. I want to make my sin look less ugly. *This* becomes my reward. Yet if we are honest, we would say we were satisfied in the moment but only for a moment. The "high" wears off quickly.

I readily admit that being right has an appeal for me. But I am learning that once gotten, it was not as fulfilling as I expected. It is similar to wanting *the toy* when I was a child. I dream of it, I think about it, I save for it, and then the day finally comes that I purchase it only to find out that it was not as advertised. It actually won't meet my *every* need.

So it is with being right, having the last word, or getting my way. They have a luring shininess to them, they do have a sense of reward in them, but let's be honest, in the end they leave us more wanting and unsatisfied.

As God has turned my heart, my affections, and my desires toward my wife for *her* benefit and *her* joy, I have realized a change in my life. The fighting urge to be right has faded and lost its importance. I cannot even tell you when it happened—it just changed. I fully recognize this was a work of the Holy Spirit in my life because I have not been that way in the past. In the past, there was more of an emphasis that *she* sees *my* point. If only that would happen, my universe would be in balance, I reasoned.

But as I view recent conversations with my wife in which we disagree on an issue, there are replies that come to mind in my own defense. The change, though, is that I do not feel the need to use them. When I could come back with a stinging statement, I am finding it is not as important to me as it once was. That burning desire has been reduced to a smoking ember. And I say an "ember" because it could easily be brought back into a flame. It is as if God is helping me to see past the situation to what a graceful and loving response would do for my marriage and how it would build my wife.

Please do not think I somehow pulled this off on my own. It was Jesus. Only Jesus. Guys, we are fooled into thinking that just keeping our mouths shut is sufficient to remedy these pressure points in our marriages. The problem with that thinking is strong discipline or willpower can keep my mouth shut. We are called to a far greater response—in fact, an *impossible* response. If it were not impossible, I could merely try harder next time. But go ahead, try on your own to change your desire within your heart. You cannot do it. That is a conversation of dependency. God, the great Vinedresser, working through the power of the Holy Spirit to overflow the fruit of looking like Jesus.

We are not asked to merely refrain from the sarcastic comment that was on our lips. Expecting the greater reward is a much higher bar. Paul reminds us in Ephesians 4:29: "Let no corrupting talk come out of your mouths, but only such as is good for building up, as fits the occasion, that it may give grace to those who hear."

The greater reward is this: when I would be satisfied with having the last stinging word with my wife, I am not only able to refrain from the carnal sarcasm but instead give words to my bride that are fitting, building, and impart grace. This applies to any area of relationship with my wife. When I could lord over her, I instead serve her. When I could posture myself to look right, I instead listen to her heart. When I could cut her down, I instead build her up. Why? *These* bring joy to a marriage. *These* speak life into a stale relationship. *These* model a pursuit that looks more like Jesus loving his church. *These* are the greater reward.

Reject passivity. Accept responsibility. Lead courageously. Expect the greater reward. These are no genie-in-a-bottle wishes for a successful marriage. Neither are they actions items on our marriage task list. They do recalibrate my thinking, though, and provide the heart postures for me to pursue. They do remind me that a full pursuit of my wife is an intentional, day-by-day, and interaction-by-interaction accumulation of choices that culminates in joy. These four ideals have not given my wife and I a rainbow-and-unicorns-no-problems marriage. What they have done is reframe how I view my marriage and remind me that I am *called* as a husband. It is a sobering reality for sure, but it is a reality that has drawn me closer to the picture that my marriage is designed to represent.

So here is what you should be asking …

COMMUNION WITH GOD: Which of the four essentials do you find most challenging to live out with your wife? Rehearse how Jesus perfectly lived out each of these.

COMMUNICATION WITH YOUR WIFE: Looking for victory? Discuss with your wife, your partner and friend, how she can come alongside you in each of these areas to encourage and build you.

COMMUNITY WITH OTHER MEN: Where are each of us finding it challenging to overflow these four qualities of Jesus before our wives?

CHAPTER 5

THE MISPLACED FEAR OF VULNERABILITY

For the last several years, I have taken a canoe/backpacking trip to Algonquin Provincial Park in Ontario, Canada, through a program called Pilgrimage. The goal is to use a wilderness experience as a tool to expose and nurture growth within its participants. The week is front loaded by immersing ourselves in a chosen passage of Scripture, getting to know our assigned teams, and spiritually readying ourselves for the week. Each leader maps out a route for his or her group. We enter the water on Monday and come out on Friday. Every year I have attended has a been a crash course in personal and spiritual growth.

This particular year I was a level-three leader, meaning that I was leading a specific group and was charged with engaging people in conversation about what they were observing in their own lives and others as seen through the grid of our selected Scripture theme. Each day involves paddling a canoe, portaging anywhere from a quarter mile up to one and a half miles to the next lake, and endeavoring to correctly read the map to get to the evening destination.

On our first day, I assigned two newbies to be the navigators. They were shown where we were on the map, but it was up to them to collaborate in navigating us through the day. They could work with others on the team as desired. We were making good time when it became apparent that we had taken a wrong spur off a lake and were lost. No signage, no landmarks, and a very tired crew. Each spur seemed to have other spurs going off, so it was difficult to navigate even how to retrace our steps.

Needless to say, there was some discouragement from my two navigators, but we processed it as a group in light of what we were learning, asked good questions, and came to some helpful conclusions.

And we eventually got back on track.

Do you feel that way as a husband? That you rub shoulders with other husbands, have some sort of "marriage map" in front of you, but do not know how to read it? You hope you are making the correct navigational adjustments, but you feel as if you are in a canoe by yourself. There are other canoes around you with husbands in them, but those guys do not feel any more confident than you do of where they are going in their marriage or how they are supposed to get there. They feel lost and are going solo.

Been there before? Yeah, me too.

It's not a great place to be. And I believe many guys are too scared to admit it. There seems to be this unwritten code of conduct that we are just supposed to know how to make our marriages work. Many men do not feel confident in their role as a husband and carry the burden of it by themselves. They have heard that they are supposed to be strong and "have it together," but if you asked them what is going on within the hidden areas of their hearts, they would admit that they are struggling, fearful, and do not know what to do.

The other half of this equation is the wife who has this "sixth sense" that something is going on with her husband, but he just will not open up about it. And this is one of the great tragedies within a marriage: the issue of vulnerability.

There is a cycle to this that we must understand if we are going to have the intimacy with our wives that both God and our wives desire. Here is how it typically works: I struggle in my life as a man and as a husband. I see my own pitfalls, and they appear ugly to me. I also see the ideals of what a husband should be and how a husband should behave. And there is a great chasm between the two. I then respond in one of two ways: I either ignore the tension going on within and think it will just go away, or I endeavor to remedy my brokenness through self-effort.

PUTTING ON A GOOD GAME FACE

I have this great fight within me to preserve face—to make sure that my wife does not see the pain going on within. She *must* not know what is *really* going on inside of me. I have this fear that in my wife *truly* and *authentically* knowing me, she would think less of me or be disappointed in me as her husband. I may fear that she would not forgive me. And I keep masking the hurt of desiring to change but not knowing how to change. I don't even understand what is going on within me and now I am supposed to let my wife into my mess?

Not a chance. Vulnerability is too difficult and too risky.

Too many guys have lived here, including myself. It can be a lonely place to be. And if you break down the situation, there is one defining thought that rises among the others: my wife will reject me if she knows the real me. And we put much effort into managing her perceptions, creating a false reality, and ignoring the pain or shame within.

This is the question that often paralyzes us: "What will my wife do with my brokenness? Will she reach out in forgiveness?"

God has worked me through this same question in more than one area of my life. It has not been easy. It has not been pleasant. But it has produced more intimacy and joy in my marriage than ever before, and I never want to go back.

But it took being vulnerable. This means that I was willing to pull back the curtain of what I was trying to minimize or hide in my life and allow my wife to fully see me. All the mess that I have falsely allowed to define me. All the shame that I have managed to suppress. All the fear that has dominated my thinking. In doing so, I realized the wall between my wife and me was of my own making. Brick by brick, over time, the wall grew thick and tall.

My flesh is masterfully devious and deceitful in this area. It pushes two distinct lies into my thinking. The first is that being vulnerable about the brokenness in my life is too hard or too risky. The second is that hiding it is the only viable solution. Both are lies but fears that can dominate us as men. It is the misplaced fear of vulnerability.

We can be paralyzed by these two mindsets because we only see our identity through the eyes of our failing performances. And though we are called to confess and repent of our sin, we are never to stay there. The reason that Jesus became *your* sin and *my* sin is so that through his mercy and grace we might become sons of God. Adopted sons means new identity. And an identity in Jesus Christ means we are no longer defined by our sin and brokenness. We are now defined by the righteousness of another.

We must back up a bit because the fruit of a lack of vulnerability may be seen in how we relate to our wives, but it is always initiated first in the relationship with our heavenly Father.

THE BIBLICAL PATH TO VULNERABILITY

In the story of King David and his relationship with Bathsheba, David tried to manage the circumstances of this tragic series of events and hide his sin. But when confronted by his prophet friend Nathan, he became honest with both himself and with his God. In Psalm 51, David lays out for us four essentials of vulnerability:

> *Have mercy on me, O God,*
> *according to your steadfast love;*
> *according to your abundant mercy*
> *blot out my transgressions.*
> *Wash me thoroughly from my iniquity,*
> *and cleanse me from my sin!*
> *For I know my transgressions,*
> *and my sin is ever before me (verses 1–3).*

First, notice that David went to God and owned his sin. He did not hide his sin because God was his solution. This is what we call full disclosure before God. No excuses, no deferring blame, no repositioning ourselves. Men, we must go to our God, and we must own our sin with him and our wives.

> *Against you, you only, have I sinned*
> *and done what is evil in your sight,*

so that you may be justified in your words
and blameless in your judgment (verse 4).

Second, though David grieved God in committing adultery with Bathsheba and killing her husband, David recognized that these things came about because of a poor view of God. David lost his awe of God and found satisfaction in himself. Likewise, *our* brokenness that we exhibit toward our wives must *first* be seen as coming from a poor view of God.

Behold, I was brought forth in iniquity,
and in sin did my mother conceive me.
Behold, you delight in truth in the inward being,
and you teach me wisdom in the secret heart.
Purge me with hyssop, and I shall be clean;
wash me, and I shall be whiter than snow.
Let me hear joy and gladness;
let the bones that you have broken rejoice.
Hide your face from my sins,
and blot out all my iniquities.
Create in me a clean heart, O God,
and renew a right spirit within me (verses 5–10).

Third, David understood that long-term change would never occur until God changed his *heart*. His heart was the primary issue and not his actions. He was fully aware that the cause of his sin came from within himself and not from the circumstances around him. God made his heart clean, and God renewed David's spirit. Though we must be killing sin within our marriages, we will never be able to fully picture Jesus and his church until our hearts are radically changed through Jesus.

In addition, notice the enormity of David's request for a solution. "Purge me with hyssop" is in reference to the tenth plague of Egypt where the Lord swept through the land, killing all of the firstborn (Exodus 12:12). Moses instructed Israel to use a hyssop branch to put blood on their doorposts so that God would pass over their homes. This was atonement for Israel as they were declared pure through no work of their own, and judgment passed over their families. David is asking God for this same extinguishing of guilt for his own sin with Bathsheba: to wipe out his sin and refuse to look at it ever again. What a bold request. This atonement is pointing to *the* Passover Lamb, Jesus, whose death puts an end to the judgment of our sin.

> *Cast me not away from your presence,*
> *and take not your Holy Spirit from me.*
> *Restore to me the joy of your salvation,*
> *and uphold me with a willing spirit.*
> *Then I will teach transgressors your ways,*
> *and sinners will return to you.*
> *Deliver me from blood guiltiness, O God,*
> *O God of my salvation,*
> *and my tongue will sing aloud of your righteousness.*
> *O Lord, open my lips,*
> *and my mouth will declare your praise.*
> *For you will not delight in sacrifice, or I would give it;*
> *you will not be pleased with a burnt offering.*
> *The sacrifices of God are a broken spirit;*
> *a broken and contrite heart, O God, you will not despise (verses 11–17).*

Fourth, complete vulnerability for David before God equated itself with full repentance. And so it does with our wives as well. Though a command, repentance is a gift and a primary step in reconciling us to our wives. And David reveals two components to repentance: a broken and contrite heart. A broken heart is a will crushed by God's grace, resulting in submission to the King and a contrite heart is a quickness or readiness to make things right. Both of these are necessary for repentance.

Did you see the phrase "joy and gladness" mixed in with "purge me with hyssop" and "let the bones that you have broken" with "rejoice"? Following his confrontation, David had no misplaced fear of being vulnerable with God. Yes,

God already knew the sin that David was hiding in his heart, but it took a process for David to honestly see himself and to see God rightly. It is worthwhile noting that David was able to be vulnerable with his God because he knew the character of his God. In one sentence David is declaring his sin, yet in the next he is rejoicing that God will forgive and renew him.

My guess would be that if you fear being vulnerable with your wife over your brokenness, there is a good chance that you also fear being vulnerable with your God. I would also speculate that if you struggle believing your wife will forgive you, you might also struggle believing that God has already forgiven you in Jesus Christ.

When we try to hide our sin and brokenness from God, it destroys all trust and intimacy with our Father. Hiding implies a poor view of God, being fearful of what he will do when he finds out what a screw-up we are. Though he will always discipline us when we rebel against him, we must not forget that he does so for our joy.

> For they disciplined us for a short time as it seemed best to them, but he disciplines us for our good, that we may share his holiness. For the moment all discipline seems painful rather than pleasant, but later it yields the peaceful fruit of righteousness to those who have been trained by it (Hebrews 12:10–11).

In a like manner, hiding who we are before our wives will greatly diminish intimacy and trust in our marriages. In fact, it's a killer. And we forget. We forget that God is wanting to work *through* our brokenness to build our relationship with our wives and take us to new levels of joy that we did not think possible.

For us as guys, our spiritual purity is so very tied to how we view our wives. Guys generally do not like to talk about purity or their failures. It's either awkward to discuss or it leads to shame. And that is among each other. It is an entirely different level when it comes to being vulnerable with our wives. Like I said before, vulnerability seems too risky. But there is also a chance we have misjudged our wives when it comes to being able to handle the truth about our brokenness.

Some years ago, I began to be unwise about where I was going on the internet. One ad or benign site led to a click that led to another link that led to a page …

that landed me on pictures that were pornographic in nature. I never *intended* to be there, but like all sin, I allowed it to mute the voice of the Holy Spirit to provide me with what I thought was better than Jesus. I was able to justify it because they were brief encounters. But after each occurrence, I felt the weight of being a son of God and choosing something other than him to satisfy me. I also felt the weight of the betrayal of the love for my wife.

I confessed and repented to God, but I knew I also needed to come clean with my wife as my burden was growing heavier and heavier. I wanted to be vulnerable and transparent with her, but my fear of her response and her rejection kept things unresolved. What would she say? Would confession just make things worse for us? What would she think of me? Would she be horribly disappointed?

I still recall the night. We were sitting in bed reading or watching some show, and the words that felt as if they were imprisoned behind lock and key finally came out. "Hey hon, I need to talk with you." With tears streaming down my face, I confessed my sin to her while feeling a weight being released within me. I asked her forgiveness. My talking stopped, and then she responded.

Her response began to put to rest my fear of being vulnerable with her. She said that she forgave me, that she would always forgive me, and that she loved me very much. It was hard for her to hear my confession, but there was mercy. The wall that I had erected of my own making was coming down quickly. I felt washed. I felt clean. I felt made whole again—both by the steadfast love of my heavenly Father and the gracious response of my wife.

This began a new depth and intimacy to our marriage relationship. It gave us open discussion about how *we* could better protect *our* marriage. In other words, she was a partner with me. She did not step on me when I stuck my neck out. She was my ally, and it produced such gratitude within me. And to this day, this is an open conversation between us in how I am doing in my own purity as well as her loving accountability with me.

That was a tough but needed lesson. And on the other side of confession and repentance was not only great joy in my marriage but an increasing victory. Today I am in a good place, and having my wife in the conversation has pushed me to better success.

WHAT IF IT DOESN'T WORK FOR ME?

I already know what some of you guys are thinking. "Yeah great, that worked for you, but you don't know my wife. This conversation would not end well for either of us." And you may be correct. Your marriage might be in a desperate place right now. Your wife may have every right to not trust you because your lack of love toward her in the past has shattered her heart. Perhaps your thirst for pornography or emotional validation from other women is still in her thoughts. Just when she thinks things are getting better, you revert back to destructive tendencies. I am not saying your wife does not have her own issues. But you have not led in sacrifice, you have loved little, you have manifested no biblical wisdom, and your wife neither feels valued nor pursued. What then?

I am humbled by my wife's grace, compassion, and forgiveness toward me. I also understand that your wife's response may be very different, and she may not want to forgive or extend mercy to you right now. The principles I am laying out for you are true but may not bring the immediate results you desire. There is no "you do this and God will do that" with sanctification. But I would encourage you that if God *is truly changing your heart's affections and desires,* be patient with your bride. Allow the gospel to continue to shape your heart posture into one that is humble, quick to repent, and trembles at God's Word. Persevere and cling to his promises for you. Serve your wife, love her, and continue speaking words of grace and living out the fruit of the Spirit. But you must be vulnerable with her because your lack of vulnerability with your wife is causing *more* danger for your marriage than your hiding is.

Perhaps you don't believe me.

Whatever the brokenness in your life, you must stop projecting your wife's response and afford her the opportunity to respond in love and grace. Listen to me. You have been deceived and in a bad way. You have allowed God's voice to become small in your life. In so doing, your wife has now been placed in enemy territory in your own mind as you make assumptions as to her response. Even *if* your wife blows up after you come clean, allow God to have his time with her. Go back to Isaiah 66:2 and remember the one whom God notices: he who is humble, quick to repent, and trembles at his word.

I would like to offer one closing thought on this topic. I was talking with a friend of mine whose marriage house is on fire. They say they want to change and do differently, but too much of their conversation involves pointing fingers at the other. As of the day we were talking, though, he said they were doing "good." The problem with that response was that, after some questioning, he admitted that "doing good" merely meant the absence of fighting, conflict, and yelling at each other.

YOU ARE NOT EVEN SURE WHAT NORMAL LOOKS LIKE ANYMORE

Here is an example. Let's say I am involved in an accident and hurt my back. I end up losing much of my quality of life. Following the injury, I have good days and bad days, meaning there are days where the pain is tolerable and I can sit and stand in spurts, while there are other days where I am laid out at home. This becomes the new norm for me. So, doing "good" on any given day does not mean a lack of chronic pain but rather that my injury has not kept me home for the day.

This is the example I gave to my friend. His marriage had been so dysfunctional for so long that he did not even know what a healthy marriage looked like anymore. His "good days" with his wife just meant they were not fighting but were speaking to each other on that particular day. His story made me both sad and angry.

Our lack of vulnerability and transparency with our wives is like having a marriage with a chronic injury. Your marriage will slowly become dysfunctional and will become defined in ways that you would not have thought possible when you said, "I do."

"We are not fighting right now."

"Things are civil."

That's a good marriage?

It is time, men. It is time to quit believing the lies of your flesh and that hiding the brokenness of your life will somehow make your marriage better or more manageable. It is time to stop being deceived that honesty will be equivalent to World War III in your home. It is time to move toward intimacy and trust. But it will begin by your laying down your fear and trusting that the Good Shepherd does not work *in spite of* our brokenness but rather *in and through* our brokenness. If Jesus is my new and truer identity, his righteousness now means I have a righteous standing before my Father. And my position in Christ and freedom in the gospel now frees me to no longer hide my sin but rather to be transparent because I am forgiven in Christ. I am his son.

So here is what you should be asking …

COMMUNION WITH GOD: How are you displaying vulnerability with your wife when it comes to your own growth in the gospel?

COMMUNICATION WITH YOUR WIFE: Do you feel as if I am open and honest with you about the struggles and sanctification in my life? What are specific suggestions you would offer me to grow in this area of being vulnerable?

COMMUNITY WITH OTHER MEN: How can the four principles in Psalm 51 help us to move to biblical transparency with our wives?

CHAPTER 6

MARRIAGE UNDER CONTRACT

Do you remember when you had this epiphany that your wife-to-be was "the one"? You probably do not recall the day or time necessarily, but do you remember when your interest in your wife went from "I really like this girl" to "I think I'm in love" to "I could spend the rest of my life with this woman!"?

Though I do not recall the day it happened for me, I do know there were plenty of moments alone where I envisioned her and I being an "us" and living out our days *together*. All I know is that I was absolutely smitten with this spunky redhead. She. Was. The. One.

I did not care where we lived or what we did for jobs as long as we were together. Sure, we had our share of conflicts that we worked through, but there was this amazing compatibility that I had never felt with any other young lady. We were a fit. We were right for each other, and there wasn't such a thing as having too much time with her. I loved the way she laughed. She was this go-getter young lady who was clearly out of my league, but one thing I knew: she loved me and I loved her.

Back in my days of college, there were no cell phones. For you younger guys reading this, stop with your look of "Seriously?". I went to a conservative Christian university where, each night, guys would run between dormitories delivering *handwritten* notes that guys and girls had written to each other—old school texting. I met my wife at college, and when we started dating, Stefanie and

I would write short notes to each other several nights of the week. I remember those euphoric moments when a note would arrive from her. To this day, I recall she sprayed her note with her perfume. You would have thought we were thousands of miles apart and I had not heard from my girlfriend in ages. I would love that time of night where I could read what she was thinking. No matter how bad the day or how stressful the class assignments, her words to me were always an encouragement and a boost.

This woman was amazing.

And to this day she has kept our notes in a box in the garage attic. Wow, talk about some blackmail material on me. Ah, those were the days.

College days ended, and I proposed to Stefanie. She had come out to California from her home in Florida, and I had this grand day planned for us. Included was a marriage proposal to her on a hill overlooking the Golden Gate Bridge.

And she said, "Yes!"

We got married and life was a dream—an extended honeymoon. We both taught at a Christian school in Florida and made very little money, but we were in love and enjoyed this new season of life called "marriage."

Fast forward five to seven years. We were living in Oregon helping in a church plant, and things began to feel *different*. I am not even sure what I mean by this term, but it is the best I can do. We still loved each other, but our marriage just sort of settled. With three kids in the mix, we loved being parents, but things between us felt sort of stale. No fighting. No daily arguments. No spending great amounts of time apart. Nevertheless, the difference between those days and the day we said "I do" was quite obvious.

So, what happened? Good question.

Many of you guys may be remiss to admit to this same problem in your marriages. It does not happen in one day or even one week. It just sort of slowly evolves, and by the time we notice its effects, it seems too late.

There is a definite dynamic that occurs, and we as husbands have to be attune to more than just its fruit because the fruit you are experiencing is merely a symptom of a heart condition that goes far deeper. I did not daily pay attention to my marriage, and as drift does, it took me to place of discouragement, frustration, and bewilderment.

WHAT A CONTRACT MINDSET WILL DO TO YOUR MARRIAGE

Some years ago, I was driving with a friend, and he said, "I want you to listen to something with me." It was a series by Andy Stanley called *iMarriage: Transforming Your Expectation.*[1] It was a three-part podcast on how sin can skew our view of our spouse. It was so impacting that I listened to the other two, we talked about them, and I have used them in premarital counseling with other couples. Andy hit the bullseye in so many practical ways as it answered marital questions that I had never verbalized. I want to lay out one of his key principles for you because it has been a game changer for me.

As men, we tend to be more process oriented: we like things laid out in a linear fashion to better understand how things operate. Inside our marriages, we often do not take the time to live with our wives in an understanding way as 1 Peter 3:7 describes. But we must come out from among the "trees" and take some time to more fully see the "forest." To not do so will result in a day-by-day, reactionary-type marriage where you wake up one day as I did and ask, "How did I get *here?*"

Every one of us went into our marriages with some sort of "here is what I hope our marriage will be like" desires and dreams. It is a good thing. It is part of the praiseworthy gift that God gives to us in anticipating what he has declared as his will and our joy. Marriage is designed by God to be nothing short of completely gratifying in him.

As time unfolds, we are tempted to give less attention to the maintenance of our marriages. To be honest, the early days of "there is a naked woman in bed with me" served as plenty of motivation to pursue my wife. We lived *together.* We did life *together.* We served *together.* The newness of matrimony was fresh and exhilarating. But as is true, if we are not giving daily energy to keeping our marriages healthy, they will never *ever* drift into anything worthwhile.

ISRAEL'S CONTRACT WITH GOD

It is at this point that a very grave thing can happen, and I want to preface it with some narrative about the children of Israel. Throughout the Old Testament, this nation's history provides such vivid and descriptive stories of a people gone bad. And yet, in reading each account, I see attitudes and perspectives that too often have become my own. Here are a few:

Now the rabble that was among them had a strong craving. And the people of Israel also wept again and said, "Oh that we had meat to eat! We remember the fish we ate in Egypt that cost nothing, the cucumbers, the melons, the leeks, the onions, and the garlic. But now our strength is dried up, and there is nothing at all but this manna to look at" (Numbers 11:4–6).

And all the people of Israel grumbled against Moses and Aaron. The whole congregation said to them, "Would that we had died in the land of Egypt! Or would that we had died in this wilderness! Why is the LORD bringing us into this land, to fall by the sword? Our wives and our little ones will become a prey. Would it not be better for us to go back to Egypt?" And they said to one another, "Let us choose a leader and go back to Egypt" (Numbers 14:2–4).

And the examples go on and on. If I put myself in Israel's "sandals," they had many desires toward their God with which I have no problem. They wanted to be delivered from slavery and go back to their homeland. They desired water and food along their journey to Canaan. They wanted protection from their enemies.

I have no issue with any of these, for they are innate desires within all of us. But something corrupt began to happen in their hearts, and it so defiled a people that the original generation was never able to step foot into their land. Over time, what they *desired* of God began to transform into an *expectation* of God.

In other words, they were presumptuous. This means that because God had said or done certain things, Israel assumed *other* intentions of God that he had not said. For example, do you recall when Israel refused to take the land of Canaan because of the giants in the land? Joshua and Caleb pleaded with the people, but they would not go. God then proceeds to tell them their unbelief has been costly: those twenty years and older would wander in the wilderness until they are all dead—they would never enter the land that God had already prepared for them to take (Numbers 14:26–35).

Israel recants. "We are sorry," they shout, "we have sinned against the Lord! We'll go take the land right now!" And the Lord replies, "Don't bother because I will not be with you." And they got their butts kicked.

It was too late. They had presumed upon God.

Throughout the storied history of Israel in the Old Testament, they displayed this mentality that had altered from a desire *for* God to an expectation *of* God. And this same mindset can easily appear in our marriages, and when it does, disaster is not far behind.

CONTRACT-TYPE THOUGHTS

We start off with good desires for our wives. We want our marriage to look and feel a certain way, but our dreams for our marriages can soon turn into rights we should expect. Have you ever thought or said any of the following?

"I have a right to be respected by my wife."

"I deserve to be treated better than this!"

"Doesn't she know that I have these needs?"

"If she would just change in this one area, it would make our marriage so much more tolerable."

"I do this for her, and she can't even (fill in the blank)?"

"Her problem is that she doesn't appreciate me—doesn't she know all I do for her?"

"I'm not the one with the problem."

The deceitfulness of expectations is that the underlying desire can be a *good* thing. It is not that what we are wanting is necessarily evil. I want to be appreciated by my wife. I want to be respected by her. Both of these are biblical desires. But the problem with expectations is that there is one way to meet them and a thousand noticeable ways not to meet them.

It becomes a checkbox with our wives. And mentally, we hold them to a standard where they must perform in order to keep us satisfied. We end up seeing them through the lens of not performing, but when they do meet our expectations, it is a ho-hum checkmark of a box.

This has happened before with regard to our sex life. I told the earlier account about how our marital intimacy had begun to subside in the throes of tiring workdays, busy schedules with the kids, and little time to ourselves. And I noticed it. It felt like we were drifting apart. Now let's pause here. Sex with my wife is a good desire. Marital intimacy between a husband and wife is designed by God and created for our pleasure. It is a wonderful gift, and God declares it to be so.

We can be easily fooled in this stage because what we desire may be a good thing. But in this season of life, there entered thoughts that at some point moved from "I would like this" to "I expect this." And from thereon out, motives would be ascribed to my wife as to why we were not having sex as frequently as I would have liked.

"Does she just not want this anymore?"

"Why is 'us' not important to her?"

"Is there something wrong with me?"

What begins to happen is a horrible spiral into a contractual relationship. What do I mean? Like you, I have vendors whom I pay for a given service each month. Let's take my internet provider. I pay a monthly fee so that I am able to have unlimited wireless access at home for all of my devices. I pay, and they provide.

There is not much to this relationship. I do not think about them often, and I would guess there is not much thought given to me as their customer. You might be an exception, but I have never called my internet provider just to tell them what a great bunch of wireless-providing-people they are. I have never emailed them to "keep up the good work" as "my wife and I have more wireless than we know what to do with!"

Sorry. Not once.

And perhaps this makes me a bad customer, but the truth is that we have an agreement—one that I signed, I might add. Do you want to guess when are the only times I call them? *When they are not meeting my expectations.* I have an expectation that I will have wireless access in my home 24/7. I do not give it much thought—at best, it is just a mental box that is checked. Most of the time I do not even think about it. In other words, there is *one* way in which I can be made happy in this relationship: provide me with wireless access. But they sure will hear from me when I have no signal in my home.

Unfortunately, at times I have taken this same mindset into my marriage, and it is corrosive to any hope of pursuing my wife like Jesus pursues his church. It will stagnate my marriage quickly. I often do not notice it because of my own self-righteous behavior. After all, shouldn't my wife and I enjoy a healthy sex life? Doesn't that please Jesus? And in my self-righteousness, I begin to ascribe both blame and motive to my wife. I have mental conversations about the way things are and what she would say if I approached her. I become the prosecuting attorney, jury, and judge, and she is found "guilty."

If you are living in a contractual relationship, you need to understand that there are three distinct areas of your marriage that will no longer exist. Stanley summarizes it well:

1) There will be no trust *in* your spouse.

2) There will be no intimacy *with* your spouse.

3) There will be no gratitude *for* your spouse.[2]

You have lost the joy of a one-flesh relationship, and you are in very dangerous territory. All you can think about is what has turned into an expectation and why your wife is in the wrong. When she meets that expectation, there is a mental "check" that it happened, but there are a hundred ways in which not to meet it. And so evidence just keeps mounting up against your wife.

No trust. No intimacy. No gratitude.

Think back to the accounts of Israel earlier in this chapter. They *expected* of God. They were tired of manna and *expected* God to give them meat. They were thirsty, and they *expected* God to meet their need right then. They frequently threw the "good ole days of Egypt" in God's face. And they were a nation who did not trust their God (Hebrews 3:19), who only knew his works and not his loving and caring father-like attributes (Psalm 103:7; Hebrews 3:7–11), and who were an ungrateful people (Deuteronomy 32:18).

I see too much of Israel in me.

If your marriage has fallen into a contractual relationship, it is not too late to be restored, though you had better see this brokenness in you with all the weight and gravity it holds because it is absolutely and completely counter-gospel.

Just the other night, in the midst of writing this chapter, I saw my propensity to do this and how things can quickly go "contractual."

As a couple, we were trying to be more intentional with our finances and where monies were being spent. We were going to initiate an auto transfer between two accounts to assist with funds we wanted to start building up. My wife said she would take care of that the next day. That next evening, I casually asked her if she had taken care of the transfer. Mind you, I decided to initiate this conversation around ten o'clock at night, after she had worked that day and then coached her varsity girls basketball game that night.

Yes, I know, stellar timing.

She said some extra things had come up in her day, and she was not able to complete the transaction. Things unraveled quickly from there. I made the very sensitive comment that it *felt* as if things I asked of her were not very important. The discussion was very conversational in tone, but the situation felt like pulling a loose string on a sweater, and before long, half of the sweater was unraveled.

Needless to say, the night did not end well. I had wounded my wife with my words by what I insinuated. Even more deeply, I realized the completion of this bank transfer had become an expectation, and all I wanted to know was if it had happened, trumping my care for her and her day. No trust. No intimacy. No gratitude. It was not the following up that was the issue. The problem was in the making much of my kingdom.

So where do you go from here? How do you move away from this contractual mindset and back into one of grace? I am going to speak to that, but first we must understand the biblical framework of a husband and wife living as one flesh because living contractually with my wife serves only to sever that union.

WHAT IT MEANS TO BE ONE FLESH

My guess is that most of you reading this book have at least *heard* the term "one flesh." Growing up, it always had this feel of mystery about it. What does it mean in the day-to-day of my marriage? Is it speaking primarily about the sexual relationship with my wife, or is there more?

To better understand this term, it is helpful to view it in its fuller context. The term "one flesh" is used six times in Scripture, and in each instance it refers to the marriage relationship. One passage that provides a helpful framework is Ephesians 5:28–33.

In the same way husbands should love their wives as their own bodies. He who loves his wife loves himself. For no one ever hated his own flesh, but nourishes and cherishes it, just as Christ does the church, because we are members of his body. "Therefore a man shall leave his father and mother and hold fast to his wife, and the two shall become one flesh." This mystery is profound, and I am saying that it refers to Christ and the church. However, let each one of you love his wife as himself, and let the wife see that she respects her husband.

In beginning to understand one flesh, we have to see it as it relates to Jesus. In the grandest picture, one flesh is representing otherworldly love: Jesus loves his church, and the church joyfully submits to Jesus as Lord. But in looking more closely at verse 31, a descriptor is used to aid us.

"Hold fast."

This term literally means to be glued together.[3] If you have ever used a substance such as super glue, you begin to comprehend its meaning. Within about thirty seconds, whatever is joined is joined for good. It is no longer two separate pieces but now one. In fact, to try to separate them after the glue has set is to risk damaging one or both of the pieces. This term is to help us better appreciate the depth, permanence, and intimacy of God's design for marriage.

The example of loving our wives is found in the way that Jesus actively loves his church: He gave himself up or committed himself to his bride for the purpose of freeing us from guilt to consecrate us to God. But then the curious phrase is used, "In the same way husbands should love their wives as their own bodies." This is written *after* the narrative of how Jesus loves his bride but *before* the use of "one flesh."

So, what does this mean, and why is it important for us as husbands? Does the author have in mind that I simply give my wife the same attention I give myself? Is this a call to not be so tied to *my* own agenda? Is this an appeal to give my marriage the same effort I give to other important areas of my life? Or is this the motivational speech of "Hey guys, since you give a lot of time and energy to your hobbies, exercising, or friendships, now it is time to suck it up and start giving that kind of attention to your wives!"

The problem I have with each of these examples is that I do not need Jesus to pull them off. These are not the fruit of heart change but the fruit of self-effort. If we are not careful, it is too easy to turn the gospel message into a moralistic "do better" type of directive. If the command sounds possible in your own strength, you have strayed from the purity of what it means to be in Christ. Oh, how we love to add our performance to the mix, thinking that Jesus + me = something better.

If you study out one flesh, "one" is not very complicated to understand in its root meaning. Ready? It means "one." It means that I am glued to my wife, and we become *one* body. So, to love my wife as I love my own body has a more rich and deep implication than merely giving more of me to my wife. For a husband to love his wife as his own body, then, must mean more than to love my wife *like* I would love my own body. I believe the essence is better found in interpreting this as loving my wife *as if* she were my own body. One flesh is not treating a second person (my wife) with the same attention I give myself. I believe this misses the marks of holding fast as well as the nourishing and cherishing that Jesus does with his church.

In addition, we can get the mistaken idea that being one flesh is my sacrificing what *I* want to do in order to do something with my wife. So, I give up mountain biking one morning to go to a farmer's market with Stefanie, all the while miserable that I cannot be doing what I *really* want to do. But hey, I am going to sacrifice to be with my wife and make her happy!

Far from it. What this actually looks like is because of the work of Jesus within me, my giving and sacrificing for Stefanie is the *very thing* that brings me joy. *Her* joy now becomes *my* joy. To make her happy is to make me happy. To bring her satisfaction is to ultimately bring me satisfaction. This is the way of living one flesh.

There is nothing wrong with my mountain biking as it is a fun and enjoyable activity to do. But I can be easily deceived that what brings ultimate satisfaction to my life is tied to me living out *my* agenda and *my* pursuits. Self-sacrifice and selfless love seem, well, too hard. We then miss the truth that the self-sacrificing love we are called to is not a grind-it-out sort of love. Let's review again how Jesus approached the mission of his Father: "Jesus said to them, 'My food is to do the will of him who sent me and to accomplish his work'" (John 4:34).

Why did Jesus serve us and sacrificially give for us? For joy. Why did Jesus endure the cross and despise the shame (Hebrews 12:2)? For joy. Do you now understand why this type of pursuit of our wives cannot nor ever will be derived of our own efforts? This type of life is beyond the bounds of possibility *unless* we have the power of another as our source: Jesus. Unless we are finding our identity *in* him. Unless our sacrifice and giving is coming *through* abiding in another. Our great joy is found *in* the serving of our wives just like Jesus's great joy is found pleasing his Father and serving his bride.

One flesh means that Stefanie's desires become my desires; her goals become my goals; what is valuable to her is valuable to me; disengaging from her is disengaging from me; and hurting her is hurting me. But most significantly, loving her is how I love myself. Paul makes this clear: "He who loves his wife loves himself." I get it—this is contrary thinking to what the culture of the world pushes at us. We are called to a love beyond "no one loves me quite like myself" or "if I don't look out for myself, no one will." This is an unattainable type of love that demands a love flowing through me that is not my own.

It is a love that can only come through a relationship that Jesus described in John 15—a vine and branch union. When Jesus proclaimed, "For apart from me you can do nothing," love was one of the fruits he was referencing. Jesus is telling us as husbands, "You want my love? Abide in me, and you will be able to love your wives with the *very same love* that I love. You want my joy? Abide in me, and you will be able to have joy in your wives with the *very same joy* that I have over you." It is the only way it can work, guys. Paul's admonition to us in Ephesians 5 is not some rally cry for us to give more effort. It is a recognition of the impossible and a submission to our Savior.

The reality of the one-flesh relationship is how we live out this pursuit of our wives, an intentional engaging, leading, and loving that is redemptive in nature, seen through the eyes of a broken steward who will one day present his bride to King Jesus. This one-flesh reality is more about the picture of Jesus and his church than it is about our marriages to our wives.

And it is the path of hope and joy. It is the path of covenantal love and not a contract.

So here is what you should be asking ...

COMMUNION WITH GOD: What does Jesus do as the bridegroom that shows his relationship to you is based on covenantal love and not a contract?

COMMUNICATION WITH YOUR WIFE: As Jesus perfectly displays covenantal love with his church, what are ways that I can actively live out covenantal love with you that make you feel valued?

COMMUNITY WITH OTHER MEN: Why does "contract" feel so natural to our hearts as men? What are you finding in the gospel that is countering this rebel heart condition?

CHAPTER 7

THE LENS OF FORBEARANCE AND GRACE

I still recall the emotion of the night as if it were yesterday, though it occurred some years ago. My wife and I were growing increasingly concerned with the struggles going on within our local church. Something was not quite right. Our souls were parched, and it was taking a toll on us spiritually.

I had never left a church in our married years, and it was a very difficult decision for me. I allowed emotions to cloud my thinking, and the decision took much longer than it probably should have. But God was both gracious and merciful in guiding my wife and I through this journey.

One night we were out with some friends driving back from dinner. We were talking through life and some of its struggles. In the background the radio was playing "Redeemed" by Big Daddy Weave. It was one of our favorite songs as a couple.

> I am redeemed, you set me free
> So I'll shake off these heavy chains
> And wipe away every stain
> Now I'm not who I used to be
> I am redeemed.[1]

In hearing it play, my wife made a comment to the effect of, "I wish our churches sang more of these types of songs because of the great reminder they provide." I assumed this was aimed at the situation with our church. It was not directed that way, but in the tension of my own heart over how to handle what was going on, that is how I interpreted it. God's direction in this decision seemed confusing at times and working through our church status became a point of irritation for me. I construed my wife's comment through a skewed lens.

In a self-preserving manner, I replied to my wife with an edge of sarcasm mixed with humor. I said something like, "Oh, don't get her started on this!" It was nothing blatant or over the top (in my estimation) but enough to make my point. And to be honest, I made my remark and moved on in my own mind. We got home that night, and my wife had her closet doors open and was facing the interior. I engaged her in some light conversation, but I was caught off guard as she was sobbing. Sensitive husband asked, "What's wrong?" Through the tears she explained how much my comment had hurt her. What she had said concerning "Redeemed" was only out of an appreciation for how God was using the song in her life and not in any way a reference to our church situation. Talk about a desperation to do *anything* to go back in time and undo words. The problem was not her comment: the issue was my failing to view her through the lens of grace.

YOU OWE ME

There is an interesting dynamic that can happen with a husband toward his wife when they are at odds over something that has either been said or done. There is this intense lust to even the score and put his world back in balance. We get entrenched in being right, getting the last word, or making the better and final point. Our emotions become so blurred and overtaken with a sense of entitlement that all we can see is where *we* are right and *she* is wrong. We see an inequity—no, we *feel* the inequity, and the scales are tipped in our favor as we take on the roles of prosecuting attorney and judge. Though we may not blurt it out, there is an attitude of "I want *mercy* for me but *justice* for her!" Sound familiar?

As husbands, we have this self-preservation instinct when our marriage relationships get out of balance. We are offended and suddenly feel the tension to get things back into equilibrium. What do I mean by this? My wife makes a comment, whether innocent or not, that sets off an alarm inside of me. I am put out, offended, or feel chafed that a criticism or observation was made of me. I have expectations for how I want to be treated, and this instance *clearly* violated those expectations in my mind.

It is similar to what happens with our bodies. If I feel myself leaning too far to the left, I compensate by leaning the other direction. If I feel as if I am falling forward, I instinctively put a foot in front of me or bring my body upright. And so it is with our marriages when in conflict. We experience this intense and burning desire to put things back in a restful state—*our* restful state. I do this through responding in a manner that repositions the argument back in my favor.

Move. Countermove.

I use sarcasm. I disengage from my wife to get back at her. I use harsh words. I spew out stinging counter examples. I defend. I defer blame. I maximize *her* failings. All of these are coping mechanisms my flesh employs to counteract the belief that I am owed and there is a debt to be paid. The frustrating thing is though there is momentary pleasure in my little kingdom-of-me being preserved and defended, there is no lasting satisfaction and the thirst within me for *me* is never quenched.

Whereas humility, contriteness, and a fear of God's words provide us with the irreducible minimum for how to view God properly, forbearance and forgiveness provide the lens through which I am able to view my wife properly in a gospel-centered way. Because what I find in my own circumstances is that it is typically not the issues themselves that keep me from reaching out in reconciliation; rather, it is the pushing away of grace and mercy that keeps me in an internal boil.[2] Mercy for *me;* justice for *her.* Sadly, in the midst of the fray, the transforming power of the gospel is the last thing I desire. What I desire is for me to feel better about me.

But the Scriptures counter this attitude. In the book of Colossians, similar to Ephesians 5, we find another mandate for how a husband is to respond to his wife: "Husbands, love your wives, and do not be harsh with them" (Colossians 3:19).

But we often miss the precursor to this command.

Put on then, as God's chosen ones, holy and beloved, compassionate hearts, kindness, humility, meekness, and patience, bearing with one another and, if one has a complaint against another, forgiving each other; as the Lord has forgiven you, so you also must forgive. And above all these put on love, which binds everything together in perfect harmony (Colossians 3:12–14).

There are two gospel-driven responses from this passage that must bookend every offense or conflict with my wife: "bearing with one another" and "forgiving each other." I am learning in new and fresh ways the transformative effects of these fruit of the Spirit in my own marriage. These are neither conflict-management skills nor ways to maintain peace in a marriage. Rather, they are heart postures born out of submission to Jesus. My desperate condition is this: my ugly responses and self-righteous actions cannot nor will not bring me the joy and satisfaction that I desire within.

Do you feel unresolvable heart tension toward your wife? Do you find yourself frustrated within and unable to release an offense that has gripped you? Can you sense the pursuit of your wife waning in the midst of yet another episode of turmoil? Is another round of offenses toward you consuming your thoughts with the evidence mounting against your wife? Then perhaps it is time to consider a new game plan: true and authentic heart change. Not "Hey hon, I'll try to be more forgiving" change. Not "Next time I'm just going to keep my mouth shut" change. If those are the responses you harbor in your heart, I can assure you that they are not of God. He does not ask you just to keep your mouth shut or to do better next time. He does ask you to confess, to repent, and to put on the fruit of bearing with your wife and forgiving her *through your identity in Jesus*. There is no other path that is going to work for you.

What is going to work is submitting to God's plan for how you engage conflict in your marriage. And there is a pre-conflict component and a post-conflict component that together will create the immense joy and gratitude in your marriage that you are desiring. On the front end I must be forbearing with my wife, and on the back end I must be forgiving with her. They work together, and the synergistic effects create a peace and love in your marriage that will transcend any of your "my little kingdom" solutions.

THE BOOKEND OF FORBEARANCE

Forbearance is not a word we use much today, so we need to unpack it to understand its marriage implications. Dave Harvey calls it preemptive forgiveness because it is a choosing of a gospel response *before an offense even happens.*[3] To be forbearing means to refrain from exercising the payment of a debt against my wife. Let's make this practical: my wife says or does something that sets me off inside. There is noise in my soul. I have taken offense, or you could say that I view her actions as a debt to be paid—she *owes* me. To exercise payment against her is to respond in such a way that settles the score or repays that debt against me. I do this in a number of ways: I disengage from her, I throw a sarcastic remark her way, I use harsh words, or I machine gun her with my seven points of why I am not wrong. Debt paid.

But in God's plan for loving my wife, he asks that I view her with the same forbearance with which God has viewed me. "Or do you presume on the riches of his kindness and forbearance and patience, not knowing that God's kindness is meant to lead you to repentance?" (Romans 2:4).

The gospel is not just what saved me. Its full and powerful effects are best seen when it engages *every* area of my life. And when I am freshly mindful that it was God's kindness that led me to repentance, it is only then I can view my wife with a right perspective—through the lens of forbearance. My exercising the payment of a debt against me only speaks to my wife that I view grace as a very small and insignificant thing and that it did not do much for me. It tells her that God's grace is not transformative *in* me but only a compartmentalized memory of what God did *for* me.

To define what forbearance is, we must also define what it is not. Forbearance is not merely acting like the offense did not happen. It is not allowing the offense to happen because to discuss the *real* problem would be too painful. It is not suppressing things within because you cannot release them to God. Forbearance is not ignoring a pattern of sin you see in your wife.[4]

"It means," says Harvey, "that you can bring love into play in such a way that you can cut someone free from their sin against you—without them even knowing or acknowledging what they've done."[5]

Cut someone free. If I believe a debt is owed to me, I will never cut my wife free. On the contrary, it becomes mission critical that she fully understand where she has offended me and how she is in the wrong. All I can see is the mounting evidence against her, and my response is craftily designed to show her that she has been declared "guilty" and must feel the weight of that guilt. If this sounds harsh, it is because it is. We can fool ourselves with thoughts of "But she …" and "I don't deserve …" statements, but the truth is that our rebel hearts have suppressed grace in order to be right.

Some reward.

Joy comes in submission. Forbearance is a fruit of the Spirit and not a switch I can flip in my heart. It means the gospel's impact in my life is overflowing to my wife before the offense ever happens. It is a Spirit-born response from abiding in Jesus. And it is freedom. I have experienced this firsthand over the last few years in my own personal growth. I no longer have that driving need to make the last and most-impacting statement. The pull of my flesh to defend or posture myself to be seen rightly is slowly dissipating. Being right is not as important to me as it once was. But I must be on guard as sin can rear its head at any time.

Jesus is clear in his teachings that my response to my wife will only create peace and harmony as I understand what God, in Christ, has done for me. If I view God's grace as a small thing, the overflow of that grace to my wife will also be small. But if I see and experience firsthand the generous and lavish nature of God's grace in my own life, it cannot help but overflow and richly influence my marriage. My response to my wife is always *first* a response to how I view what God has done for me. This is why a right view of God will always precede a right view of my wife.

Do you remember the story in Luke 7 about Simon the Pharisee? He had Jesus and some others over for a meal in his home. In all his days of hosting guests, none held his attention like Jesus. Everything is going well until a woman walks into their midst. And not just any woman, but she is described as a sinner. This word has implications that she was disdained. She was seen as preeminently sinful and especially wicked, stained with certain vices that led her onlookers to believe that her very life was devoted to sin.[6]

It was bad enough that a woman with this sort of reputation walks into Simon's house, but she begins to cry, and her tears roll off the feet of Jesus. She dries his feet with her hair and then finishes her display of affection and submission by anointing Jesus's feet with an expensive perfume.

This party just came to a screeching and awkward halt.

It is interesting that Simon's first thought goes to Jesus. "If he were the prophet he claims to be," thought Simon, "he would know that he should not allow this sort of woman to be touching him. She is a sinner, and it is inappropriate."

If you recall this narrative, Jesus answers Simon's concern with an indicting story of two men who owed money to a bank. One owes a smaller sum, and another owes ten times the amount. Neither can pay their debt. The banker, out of mercy, cancels the debt of both men. They are free and clear—debt paid. Jesus asks Simon, "If both have their debts cancelled, which of the two will be more grateful?" "The one who had the bigger debt cancelled, I suppose," Simon says.

Jesus's story could not have been clearer or more incriminating of Simon. Jesus forgives the sins of this sinful woman, and it disgusts Simon. He cannot understand why this woman would fall over Jesus or why Jesus would entertain such behavior. Simon had no category for grace. But Jesus's message is clear: this woman experienced firsthand the effects of grace and forgiveness in her life, and it overwhelmed her. Her over-the-top display of gratitude was in response to the over-the-top grace she had received.

As a husband, I am more like Simon than I care to admit. The effects of grace are, at times, seemingly small in my personal life, so its overflow is small in my marriage.

Think through what generates conflict in your marriage. How much of the rising stress is due to your need to exercise payment of the debt for what your wife said or did to you even before the offense has occurred? My guess is quite a bit because I see it in my own marriage. But imagine how a situation could be immediately defused because of the forbearance you displayed toward your wife as a conflict was beginning. And not only that, imagine how your wife would then see you modeling Jesus in a way that looks like Jesus pursuing his church?

This is one way in which we can lead our wives: by living out before them the forbearance, grace, and love that has been lavished on us from God in Christ.

This is not a "just suck it up and be civil to your wife." These types of responses can only come as we first recognize the standing that we have as sons of God and are overtaken by gratitude for such an underserved position of favor. As I consider passages such as Psalm 103 and God's as-high-as-the-heavens-are-above-the-earth steadfast love or his as-far-as-the-east-is-from-the-west forgiveness, the Spirit shapes my heart posture, and it becomes one that displays forbearance to my wife. Why? Because when I view Stefanie, I remember that *she also* is participating in the glorious workings of the gospel as a daughter of God. If I have been richly influenced by the thought of God's being forbearing with me, how can I not display that attitude in how I relate to my wife?

Do you now see why a right view of my wife can only come through a right view of my God? A lack of forbearance in how I respond to my wife is a tangible expression of an eroding relationship with God—that *my* sins are small compared to hers and that she deserves much less grace than *I*. Conversely, a display of forbearance toward my wife in the midst of an offense is a tangible expression of abiding in Jesus as the vine. Remember, "for apart from me," Jesus asserts, "you can do nothing."

THE BOOKEND OF FORGIVENESS

Forgiveness is then the other bookend that surrounds an offense in grace. Unlike forbearance, forgiveness is a more common word, though we may be viewing it as less than what it is. Whereas forbearance is a refraining of the exercise of a debt, forgiveness is a free or gracious release. Harvey says, "[Forgiveness] requires that you absorb certain effects of another person's sins and you release that person from liability and punishment."[7]

In biblical forgiveness, I may still feel the pain of the offense debt against me. But in forgiving, I am choosing to absorb the consequences of my wife's actions or words and not demand that she experience *my* heartache and hurt in return. I will not bring it up again, and I will not force her to relive it. I release her in the same way that the gospel has released me.

If I am desiring my wife to feel a pain equal to my own, I have not forgiven her. The offense so dominates my thinking that I am unable to treat her as Jesus has treated me. The magnitude of the offense rings louder and truer than the opportunity for grace. I forget that she is also participating in the daily process of being made to look more like Jesus.

> *When my mind is fixed on the gospel, I have ample stimulation to show God's love to other people. For I am always willing to show love to others when I am freshly mindful of the love that God has shown me. Also, the gospel gives me the wherewithal to give forgiving grace to those who have wronged me, for it reminds me daily of the forgiving grace that God is showing me.*

> *Doing good and showing love to those who have wronged me is always the opposite of what my sinful flesh wants me to do. Nonetheless, when I remind myself of my sins against God and of His forgiving and generous grace toward me, I give the gospel an opportunity to reshape my perspective and to put me in a frame of mind wherein I actually desire to give this same grace to those who have wronged me.[8]*

The sad story is there are too many times where I do not want to give forgiving grace to my spouse. I am more concerned that she feels the pain exacted to me. Did you note the condition in the prior quote? "When my mind is fixed on the gospel …" These are important words, for they define the heart posture that must be present in order for forgiveness to occur. As with a lack of forbearance, a lack of forgiveness stems from a small view of God that manifests itself in a desire for fairness over forgiveness.

Let me ask you a couple of questions. But first, think about your wife. Is there any tension when you think about her, any noise that you find in your soul over an offense that you just cannot release? Do your thoughts wrap around this event or series of events that you believe she has initiated? Have you had trouble forgiving her, releasing her from having to experience the same pain and frustration that you have felt from her? In other words, is it difficult to forgive?

Now put your thoughts on God. How is your relationship with Him? Is it vibrant and fresh, and are your thoughts saturated in his promises? If the above scenario is true regarding your wife, my guess is "no." In fact, if this is true, it is impossible that you can have a proper view of your God. This is true because Scripture is clear that what *I* do is always in response to what *he* has done. "Let all bitterness and wrath and anger and clamor and slander be put away from you, along with all malice. Be kind to one another, tenderhearted, forgiving one another, as God in Christ forgave you" (Ephesians 4:31–32).

I am not simply told to be forgiving with my wife. I am to be forgiving with my wife *as God in Christ forgave me.* Without this emphasis, I am left with just trying to let offenses go. No, rather the calling and the opportunity are much greater. As Jesus said to Simon, "He who is forgiven much, loves much and he who is forgiven little, loves little." My inability to forgive my wife is never accompanied with lofty thoughts of all of which God, in Christ, has forgiven me. In fact, in that moment when my lack of forgiveness is looming, what God has done for me seems inconsequential.

"As God, in Christ, has forgiven me." *This,* and only *this,* is what allows me the opportunity to freely give to my wife and release her. "If one has a complaint against another, forgiving each other; as the Lord has forgiven you, so you also must forgive" (Colossians 3:13).

GRACE, NOT JUST IN OUR MARRIAGE

I want to tell you about one of the more impacting seasons in my marriage. It may not seem to be related to pursuing my wife, but hang with me because I will get there. When my son was in high school, I had the privilege to be his basketball coach, which allowed me to be more involved with his life. I desired that he be a godly young man in pursuit of Jesus. But as I began to view him, I became suspicious of behaviors and found myself "sniffing out smoke to find the fire."

"What music are you listening to on your iPhone?"

"Why are you looking at that girl?"

"Are you having your devotions?"

I had trained my son all these years, and I had forgotten there needed to come a time when I put more trust in *his* decisions and to support *him* in his desires and goals. I was not doing that. I was wanting control.

Though my end goal may have been noble, my lack of forbearance and grace toward him only revealed my heart to control how he turned out. When I felt as if he was not getting my point, I would reinforce it with a witty or sarcastic remark in order to regain (what I interpreted as) being in control.

My son began to date a young lady his senior year in high school, and this pattern would emerge from time to time in our relationship. Though living in our home, he was not sure how to approach me about what he was experiencing between us and would confide in my wife. She would then talk with me. The conversational triangle.

During their time of dating, I recall my son and his girlfriend coming to speak with me about some challenges they were facing as a couple. I was very grateful they spoke with me, and I went home that night to speak with my wife. In my own struggles of control and walking through one of my children dating for the first time, my initial response was to take the easier path and be done with the dating relationship. But as I spoke to my wife, we found ourselves asking the question, "What would grace look like with our kids in this situation? And how would we go about showing that?"

We prayed, we talked, and we prayed some more. And in the end, we both felt a working of the Holy Spirit in our hearts to reach out to our son and his girlfriend in grace and walk this journey with them. In speaking with them, they both requested to be discipled by my wife and I and that we help them to navigate this piece of their relationship.

And so Stef and I began to meet with them: me with my son and my wife with his girlfriend. God began to mature them and grow them, and he grew my wife and I in new and amazing ways. It was like the question of "What does grace look like?" was repeatedly being asked of us, and all we knew was to turn to God to drive the affections of our hearts. In the midst of all of this, the relationship between my son and I was not fully repaired yet. And my son's girlfriend knew as well that things were not quite right. Needless to say, it put a strain on the dynamics of desiring to reach out to my son's girlfriend and make her part of the family. I recall one night that they both were over to the house. Earlier that day, my son and I were in conversation about something in which I began to feel I was losing control of the situation and resorted to sarcasm instead of grace. My wife mentioned this to me once again and expressed her concern in how I was working through this.

I want to pause this story for a moment. I hope you realize that part of God's manifested grace in our lives is his allowing us as sons to experience the epic fail of resolving conflict outside biblical principles. In other words, God's working does not just include moving us to repentance but also allowing us to taste the fruits of our own self efforts. I say this is grace because God does not have to allow us the bitter taste of doing life without him. But he does, and we end up being overwhelmed by his grace to lead us to repentance and restore what we could never have restored ourselves.

This is what God did for me. It was like my eyes were veiled by my lack of grace because all I could see was the "what" and did not care about the "how." And it was in that moment that God pulled back the veil of my spiritual eyes and I saw specifically what it was I was doing to my son and his girlfriend. God knew my heart was ready and showed me *my* ugliness in order to experience *his* beauty. I saw firsthand what I had been doing, and it leveled me.

I confessed. I repented. I told God that, by his grace and power, this pattern would be done in my life, and I reached out to my heavenly Father to help me. Later that night I pulled my son and his girlfriend into my bedroom to speak with them. With tears streaming down my face, I asked their forgiveness and confessed that my lack of grace toward them was sinful. It was wrong, and these types of responses were going to stop immediately through God's help.

I am not sure that they fully knew what to do with this, but God began to heal our relationships. I recall some months later when my son and I were walking together, and I told him again how sorry I was for that period in our lives. His response was remarkable: "Dad, that's been forgiven and is behind us now. Let's walk in the new relationship we have together."

Fast forward and my son ended up marrying that very same young lady. Though she is technically my daughter-in-law, I only speak of her as my third daughter. She is the perfect complement to my son, and she has brought much joy to our family. I love her dearly, and she brings a smile to my heart. My son and I have an amazing relationship between us, and I give all my gratitude to God. I admit there are times when I am tempted to think or respond to something in a non-grace-like manner, and I am immediately reminded of what God gave back to me. God is still teaching me.

I know this story may seem out of place in a book on marriage for guys but allow me to explain. That season of time in the life of my wife and I was far more impacting than just in rearing our kids. God worked grace-filled responses into both of our lives and helped us to understand how that same forbearance and forgiveness is to overflow to each other. These "bookends" have transformed us as a couple and drawn us together in ways that I could have never imagined.

I AM THE CHIEF OF SINNERS

My greatest enemy is within *me*—it is not my wife. As long as you believe the greatest faults always lie with your wife and she is the reason for your screwed-up marriage, you will continue to drift apart. Reconciliation will never become reality. I must grasp that my greatest enemy is within me, and my wife must also grasp that her greatest enemy is within her. Until that happens, expect the turmoil to continue. But I can speak from experience that God only wants to expose my enemy within in order to help me to obtain the full joy that I am seeking and see *him*. Except the full joy I am craving is not in being right with my wife or winning the argument with my wife. It is serving her in a heart posture of forbearance and forgiveness, and only God can bring that about.

There may be some of you as husbands who are thinking, "God *has* changed me, and I am now showing forbearance and forgiveness, but it is making no difference in our marriage."

Be longsuffering and patient, my friend. If you have been a failing example of a husband in the past, there may be some skepticism on the part of your wife if she has heard empty promises before. "But God *has* changed me!" you might say, and perhaps he has. Again, endure. Do not presume on God and make the assumption that because you changed, your wife should immediately be changed as well. Allow God to write the narrative of your story and do not add your own qualifiers. Realize you now have sown the seeds to reconciliation and restoration and that *he* and *he alone* will do the work. You have responded in obedience so now allow God to reconcile hearts. In the meantime, pursue her. Pursue her with a spirit of forbearance and pursue her with a response of forgiveness. She will notice. And when she does, prepare to view a marriage being transformed.

So here is what you should be asking …

COMMUNION WITH GOD: What type of situations with your wife cause you to view her as being "in debt"? How does God's freeing you of the debt you owed to him change the way you view each of these situations?

COMMUNICATION WITH YOUR WIFE: In response to my own reflection, I realize there are areas in which I do not have a heart posture toward you of forbearance and am holding you "in debt." In viewing God's grace as insignificant in my own life, I have failed to overflow grace into your life. Will you forgive me for _____ and allow the gospel to reconcile our hearts?

COMMUNITY WITH OTHER MEN: How is what God has done in Christ for us the foundation for showing true forbearance and forgiveness to our wives?

CHAPTER 8

THE HOLY INTIMACY IN MARRIAGE

Yes, the sex chapter, men. We are finally going to address it. For many of you as husbands, there are two thoughts that may have passed through your minds: 1) Why did it take Antone so long to get to this chapter? and 2) Why not make this a one-chapter book and be done with it?

I make those comments somewhat facetiously, but I know this tends to be a relevant topic among guys in marriage—yet one that is not getting addressed as it ought. I grew up in a conservative circle, and the topic of sex was never brought up. It was always sort of this Christians-don't-talk-about-this subject matter, and as a young man I noticed that no one, and I mean no one in our circles, dared discuss the idea of sexual intimacy from a biblical perspective. Even the Song of Solomon was this it's-in-the-Bible-but-let's-pretend-it's-not sort of book. In Sunday School classes, we zipped through saying our Old Testament books of the Bible: "… Job, Psalms, Proverbs, Ecclesiastes, Song of Solomon …" but we never seemed to have any stories from *that book,* the Song of Songs. I can only imagine the hoopla it would have caused to have my teacher illustrating "Your two breasts are like two fawns, twins of a gazelle" on her flannelgraph board. "So, when was Mrs. Johnson's last day teaching Sunday School? Oh yeah, the fawn incident."

If sexual intimacy is never really addressed from a biblical perspective, it is too easy to come away with a mentality of "sex is bad" or, at minimum, something we should not talk about. We see its perversions in society, but it is addressed far too infrequently in Christian circles. Or, should I say, it is seldom discussed within a biblical framework. Our culture implies great sex is what happens outside of marriage while marital sex is left to seem dull with an "I'm too tired" feel to it. And unfortunately, men, and the husbands they become, are left to figure it out on their own because no one is teaching them what God says about holy sex and the role it should play *in marriage.* This ends up being tragic because if not biblically taught, husbands end up with a very skewed view of sex, embracing a dysfunctional mindset of something that was designed to be a gift of God and a pure joy in marriage.

This chapter is not a warning against pornography and its dire effects on men in our local churches. We've all heard it, and it is true. It is not to present the stats on the number of husbands who call themselves believers who are wrecking their marriages in emotional or physical affairs. We get it, and it is also true. Rather, this chapter is a declaration that sex between a man and his wife is a *good thing* and was created to bring glory to God. We forget that sex was God's idea. It was not some consequence of man's fall in the garden of Eden. "And Adam, because you have disobeyed my words, the ground is cursed, you will eat by the sweat of your brow, and you will have to have sexual relations with Eve all the days of your life." No, a man's pleasure in sexually pursuing his wife is something blessed by God. He thought of it. He designed it. He calls it good *within the parameters that he has set up* for our enjoyment and his glory. But you will never drift there. It takes a lot of intentional and daily initiative.

SEX IS MORE THAN JUST ... SEX

Though our society has made sex "the first chapter," I have specifically placed it at the end by design. Like so much of my role as a husband, a sexual relationship with my wife is more of a heart posture before my God than it is an act with my wife. Our culture tells us that sex is what initiates love; God says it is the fruit of love. I have spent some considerable time in this book working through what it means for a man to pursue his wife as Jesus pursues his church. If this is true in your life, your sex life is going to be an amazing overflow of God transforming your life to look more like Jesus. And if this is not true in your life, your sex life is going to be a physical manifestation of the frustrations and tensions going on in your heart.

Somewhere along the way, sexual intimacy got separated from the mandate to be "conformed to the image of his son" (Romans 8:29). Somewhere along the way, sexual pleasure with my wife became a hushed topic from other elements of biblically loving my wife. It is like the whole sex thing is assumed to be common knowledge among husbands—not the physical act itself; no, rather its place in the pursuit of my wife. And in our parenting and churches, we have missed a beautiful opportunity to help young men understand the gift of sex and how it can be used to serve their wives.

Unfortunately, what is not discussed in biblical community is often pursued in secret, and a husband's knowledge of sex with his wife is sourced in what he has learned from pornography or simply flying blind. John Piper makes an excellent observation when he says:

> *You don't have to be an ascetic, and you don't have to be afraid of the goodness of physical pleasure, to say that sexual intimacy and sexual climax get their final meaning from what they point to. They point to ecstasies that are unattainable and inconceivable in this life. Just as the heavens are telling the glory of God's power and beauty, so sexual climax is telling the glory of immeasurable delights that we will have with Christ in the age to come. There will be no marriage there (Matthew 22:30). But what marriage meant will be there. And the pleasures of marriage, ten-to-the millionth power, will be there.[1]*

This chapter is not just addressing the elephant in the room—but the *awkward* elephant in the room. I believe guys *want* to have discussions about this topic, and I believe guys *want* to understand its biblical role in marriage but have no idea how. And so marriages continue to suffer. And I would like to add that I do not believe that sex is the end-all of marriage. It is not the reason my marriage exists, and it is not the waking thought of every day. But it does play a significant role, and a more biblical perspective of intimacy with my wife has radically transformed our marriage and can radically transform your marriage.

Near to the time of writing this chapter, my wife spoke individually with three discouraged wives, and in each case there was at least some discussion about their sex lives. In two of the conversations, each wife spoke of how exhausted they were in life, and yet one constant was that their husbands wanted more sex with them. They just were not as excited about it as their husbands. In the other instance, a woman was pouring out her heart to my wife about her marriage. My wife asked her, "So how is your sex life?" and the woman broke down and began to cry. She was angry with her husband and stated that he was not deserving of having sex because of how he treated her. He was distant and unengaged. So how does a couple come together and have a mutual understanding about a subject that God declares to be good but yet can be the source of so much angst and frustration?

ACTUALLY, SEX WAS GOD'S IDEA

To begin we must understand what God says, not just about marriage, but about a sexual relationship inside the covenant of marriage. There is not an abundance of passages about the physical relationship between a husband and wife, but there are enough to guide us in our thinking and lay out a roadmap for us. Here are three: two from the Old Testament and one from the New Testament.

Let your fountain be blessed, and rejoice in the wife of your youth, a lovely deer, a graceful doe. Let her breasts fill you at all times with delight; be intoxicated always in her love (Proverbs 5:18–19).

You have captivated my heart, my sister, my bride; you have captivated my heart with one glance of your eyes, with one jewel of your necklace. How beautiful is your love, my sister, my bride! How much better is your love than wine, and the fragrance of your oils than any spice! Your lips drip nectar, my bride; honey and milk are under your tongue; the fragrance of your garments is like the fragrance of Lebanon. A garden locked is my sister, my bride, a spring locked, a fountain sealed. Your shoots are an orchard of pomegranates with all choicest fruits, henna with nard, nard and saffron, calamus and cinnamon, with all trees of frankincense, myrrh and aloes, with all choice spices—a garden fountain, a well of living water, and flowing streams from Lebanon. Awake, O north wind, and come, O south wind! Blow upon my garden, let its spices flow (Song of Solomon 4:9–16).

The husband should give to his wife her conjugal rights, and likewise the wife to her husband. For the wife does not have authority over her own body, but the husband does. Likewise the husband does not have authority over his own body, but the wife does. Do not deprive one another, except perhaps by agreement for a limited time, that you may devote yourselves to prayer; but then come together again, so that Satan may not tempt you because of your lack of self-control (1 Corinthians 7:3–5).

In each of these sections of Scripture, the narrative is straightforward that a sexual relationship between a husband and wife is a good and godly thing. It is not frowned upon or discouraged but rather celebrated. And let's be clear—if there is tension in your marriage over this topic, my guess is it is not over your *wife* desiring to have more sex with you. I have never, in all my days of discipling husbands, had a guy express, "Sheesh … my wife wants to make out all the time!" No, the tension that accompanies this aspect of marriage usually manifests itself in private frustration where the husband feels awkward talking about their sex life, and the two are on very different pages when it comes to sexual intimacy.

The sexual intimacy that God has declared to be a good thing between a married couple has some qualifiers that are too often forgotten in a marriage. And if those qualifiers are ignored, intimacy between a husband and wife will fall into disarray. There was a time earlier in my marriage where I did not understand the core ideas of this chapter, and consequently, I ended up with a skewed view of sex that became unhealthy and unbiblical. And guys, understand this: a declining sexual relationship with your wife is typically one of the final fruits to appear in a poor marriage relationship. By the time a husband thinks, "What has happened to our sex life?", there are usually several red flags that have been ignored leading to that point. In other words, as Dennis Rainey has said, sex is more of a thermometer in my marriage than a thermostat.[2] Disengaging from a wife, less interest in her desires, lack of pursuit, minimal conversation, a defensive heart posture, harsh words—many to all of these have already been in play long before a couple's sexual intimacy fades away or becomes nonexistent.

As husbands, we must not forget the law of sowing and reaping. Paul exhorts in Galatians 6:7 to "… not be deceived: God is not mocked, for whatever one sows, that will he also reap." There have been seasons of my marriage where I have been disappointed and discontent with how things were going in the sexual intimacy department. What I failed to see was that my current condition was not based on current habits or actions. Rather, my current condition had been years in the making. It was an accumulation of many daily decisions, responses, and heart attitudes over time whose fruit I was left to eat.

As I mentioned earlier, I placed this chapter toward the end of this book by design. Sexual intimacy with my wife should also be an expression of how I pursue my wife like Jesus pursues his church. And to pursue her with the right heart posture, I must understand and live out several key ideas discussed in previous chapters: God takes note of the one who is humble, quick to repent, and fears God's words; his identity is found in Jesus; he is vulnerable with his wife and guards against a contractual relationship; and he lives out the biblical view of being one flesh and overflows forbearance and forgiveness into all conversations and experiences with his bride. *These* are what prepare for a healthy, vibrant, and satisfying sex life with my wife. To separate sexual intimacy from the biblical heart posture of being a husband in full pursuit moves sex from being an expression of serving my wife to simply being a base act or a "need" that I have—an expectation.

Serving your wife in your sexual intimacy—does this concept seem foreign to you? Or perhaps you have just forgotten. This is one of the consequences of men not discussing these things in biblical community or getting into God's Word: sex becomes this stand-alone act that is severed from God's design of serving and loving my wife in *all* areas of my marriage. And when I sense my sexual life is disappearing, both anxiety and apathy will invade the relationship. Anxiety because of what I am not getting. Apathy because I don't know what to do and quit caring.

My marriage, as of the writing of this book, is in the best place it has ever been in our twenty-nine years of matrimony, and that includes our sexual life. My marriage is amazingly wonderful, but it is hard work. And it is not just hard work, but every-day-in-all-the-little-stuff hard work. We did not coast into it, and we did not drift to this point. Back in chapter 4, I told the story of "the restaurant conversation." Our intimacy had gotten stale over time, and I began to come to poor conclusions as to why—all related to my wife. In relaying this to my wife over breakfast at the Amberg Cafe, her response was, "Why don't you just pursue me?" I was not expecting that response, and what she said clearly put the ball back in my court. This is not how this conversation was supposed to go, or so I thought.

As part of this breakfast chat, she also made another revelation to me. What she said stung, but after my initial defensiveness subsided, I realized it was true. She told me that sexual intimacy was not as desirable as it once was because she began to view it as my expectation of her. "This is what good wives do." She also conveyed that she felt as if I only showed interest in her when I wanted to make love. Ouch. Wasn't expecting that one. And that my pursuit of her was only to meet a sexual "need." Okay, I think we're done here. I heard her out but came away with a sense of "Wow, didn't see that one coming—at all."

I remember praying to God and telling him that, in all honesty, I did not know *how* to pursue my wife like he desired. I needed him to change my desires and affections and put within me something I could never manufacture. I repented to my wife and to God and asked for him to intervene. The end result of that prayer was not a great sex life. Rather, it was a shaping of a heart posture that began to more frequently have my wife in my "crosshairs," to listen to her heart, and to serve her. And I realized that serving my wife in a Jesus-type manner also included our sexual relationship. Though sex gave *me* much pleasure, my serving *her* in our intimacy accomplished three amazing things: it brought glory to God, it brought satisfaction to my wife, and in turn, gave me much pleasure. It was what God did in me *first* that produced a sexual experience that was wonderfully satisfying for both of us.

Since that time, God has continued to refine both my thinking and my actions. Oh, I still display plenty of brokenness on a regular basis. But my wife knows she is in my clear focus and has communicated that to me. A dear friend of mine told me that every time he passes his wife, in his home or in public, he touches her. I have always remembered that. God is continuing to give me affections and desires for my wife, and it is in the daily life touches that I am led to love Stefanie more and better, which results in desiring to serve her in our sexual intimacy. Our intimacy is simply another display of my pursuing her like Jesus pursues his church.

There is one other important consideration found in 1 Corinthians 7:5, and it is immensely practical: "Do not deprive one another, except perhaps by agreement for a limited time, that you may devote yourselves to prayer; but then come together again, so that Satan may not tempt you because of your lack of self-control."

In Ephesians 6, Paul instructs believers to employ the shield of faith to defeat the enemy. And in 1 Corinthians, he tells believers to have frequent sex to fight against sexual temptation. "Faith makes use of sexual intercourse as a means of grace," says Piper, and "sexual relations are a God-ordained means of overcoming temptation to sin."[3] I can affirm this from my own marriage. Sexual intimacy with my wife is extremely helpful in warding off lustful desires. My sexual satisfaction with her generates an equal dissatisfaction for the pursuit of lustful thoughts, that extra click on the internet, or lingering on a sensual program. That is not to say that I do not fight lust because I do every day, but a sanctified sexual life with my wife has sanctified me in other areas of my life. My wife knows this, and in serving each other in intimacy, we know we are helping to protect our marriage and bring more glory to God.

And allow me to insert one additional thought here. When I am not satisfied in Jesus and my bride, I will inevitably look to *something* to satisfy. *This* is the stage where danger is first present, not in the act of doing. Pornography, an emotional affair, or physical adultery are all soul-sucking replacements because we are hardwired to be in awe. Though the joy comes in being in awe of Jesus, we are mesmerized with sly offerings of our flesh *for something better*. This is why we must fight for our satisfaction in Jesus and in our bride. As a friend once told me, "Our eyes must starve for our wife alone."

INTIMACY IS MORE THAN JUST SEX

So, you might ask, "How do you *serve* your wife in sexual intimacy?" First of all, you must ask some questions of her. For most of us as guys, intimacy is equated with sex. Umm, what else is there? But it would be wise of you to ask your wife how *she* defines intimacy. You may be surprised that she has many answers other than "sex." I have asked my wife this question. She told me that intimacy to her does include our sexual relationship, but it also includes sitting close to her, touching her often, snuggling on the couch watching her crime show dramas, and listening to her heart and not just her words. This was such a helpful conversation because these are ways to serve her as she views intimacy. And realize that intimacy with your wife, even sexual intimacy, may change as you both get older or enter new seasons of life. When my wife sees an authentic expression of love in the form of service, sex becomes just one more expression of how I serve my wife. Sex becomes more than some base need; rather, a sexual relationship is more about my showing love to her and telling her how there is no one I desire other than her. Her excitement is my excitement. Her climax is the goal and not my own.[4]

Peter makes an insightful statement when he says in 1 Peter 3:7, "Husbands, live with your wives in an understanding way." To live in an understanding way with my wife has the idea of dwelling with her in both a domestic and sexual way that leads to wise living.[5] It is important that we understand what Peter is saying in this narrative. I live with her according to my knowledge of her. And to do this demands I listen to her, observe her, and pursue her. It means I live with her in a way that helps her walk with Jesus, makes her holy, and models repentance and reconciliation to her.

This is the way of the gospel. The most significant aspect of my marriage is not so much Stefanie and me but rather displaying the picture of Jesus and the pursuit of his bride. He is relentless. His love is steadfast, his forgiveness is boundless, his motives are always for my good, and his discipline always yields the peaceable fruit of righteousness. My hope is that God reveals new and better things to you about the sexual intimacy you can have with your wife. It was designed by God to be good, holy, and lived out in faith. And as he realigns your heart, I believe you will see great things happen in your shared intimacy. But my caution to you is to be patient. God is the one who changes hearts. We give mental assent to this, but it is difficult to live out because we think *our* change should then produce *her* change ... now. She may respond with gratitude and excitement, but she also may be a bit gun-shy based on your past or simply resistant. Show a gentleness and quietness in your spirit. Keep the dialogue fresh and keep it frequent. Pray for her and with her. Allow your intimacy to be a by-product of your full pursuit of her.

So here is what you should be asking …

COMMUNION WITH GOD: Why is a heart posture of service so necessary for a fulfilling sexual relationship with your wife?

COMMUNICATION WITH YOUR WIFE: How would you personally define intimacy? How would you describe our spiritual, emotional, and sexual intimacy? What growth would you like to see between the two of us in these areas?

COMMUNITY WITH OTHER MEN: What can we do as men to push each other to a godly pursuit of our wives in this area of intimacy? What do we need to put off (lust, pornography, emotional affairs, thought patterns, etc.) in order to put on hearts that pursue our wives spiritually, emotionally, and physically?

CHAPTER 9

GETTING THERE

The prayer for this book is to prod you to new thinking and realign your thoughts as it relates to this most amazing of earthly relationships called marriage. I have written it for three types of husbands. To husband #1: perhaps your marriage is off the charts awesome right now. To you I would say, "Press on and allow King Jesus to keep shaping you as a husband. Be the type of man to whom God will look: humble, quickly repenting, trembling at the words of God." Use this text and its questions as talking points with your wife to keep things fresh as well as to have frequent recalibration.

To husband #2: perhaps when thinking of your marriage, things seem manageable. You have some communication issues between you, but no one is yelling. They certainly are not as bad as what you see in *other* couples. Things are stale and your marriage is dysfunctional, but the problem is that you have gotten used to it and, over time, no longer recognize what a godly and healthy marriage looks like. Your marriage has not fallen off the cliff though you would admit that you are dissatisfied. Your wife has expressed a desire for you to initiate and pursue her more like Jesus, but your work life, hobbies, or "life of ministry" is what feels more natural. You attribute your wife's sentiments to being a bit reactionary or just the way she is. Change for you involves addressing matters when your wife hits a certain level of emotion. "Sorry, hon," you might say, "I'll try not to do that next time."

To you I would say, "You are heading for a crisis. Like lying back in a canoe that follows a lazy river, you are getting lulled to sleep because you are not anticipating any danger. While you are asleep in your canoe, you fail to notice the dangerous whirlpool that will cast you into the rocks and pull you under." Do you want this to change? Please read on.

To husband #3: perhaps the thought of your marriage causes you deep pain, agony, frustration, or sorrow. You don't know where things went off the rails or when, but you are staring at one enormous display of brokenness and have no clue how to get yourself out of the pit of your own making. I get it—the relational strain seems so great that hope for a new norm is waning or seems nonexistent. You desire your relationship with your wife to be anything other than what it is, but there is a heavy weight inside and all your thoughts end in desperate attempts to make things right.

To you I would say, "I am encouraged, my friend. You need to get to the end of your rope. Now you are ready for Jesus to do what only he can do: change the affections and desires of your heart and reshape your marriage." Have you ever thought about the fact that being brought to the end of yourself is an act of grace and mercy by your loving Father? Really, it is. Why? Because if I were never brought to the end of myself with all its broken thinking and sinful actions, I would keep on believing *my* efforts and strategies could fix my marriage. I would continue to be lulled into a state of slumber thinking my marriage isn't as bad as it actually is and that circumstances or people other than me are to blame. If my greatest fullness of joy is found in my identity with Jesus, and it is, then it is an act of his lovingkindness to move us to the place where we cry out, "God, I surrender. Would you do something, *anything,* to help my marriage? I have made a mess of things. I am completely dependent on you."

God's mercy is in your mess. I know, your situation with your wife may be anything but an aroma of grace right now. But God is present even in *this.* He is about your reconciliation because reconciliation is one of the strongest messages of the gospel. God is a covenant-keeping God, and if you are one of his adopted sons, he faithfully came after you when you were not faithfully going after him. He is the rescuer from sin and death, and he longs to be the rescuer of your marriage. He wants to do this because it brings him glory, and it brings you the joy after which you have been chasing.

If God did not bring you to the end of yourself, imagine the despairing situation that would be. But God, in his love, grace, and discipline, allows you to see your sin, not to shame you but to reveal Jesus. *He* is your answer. God does not "rub our noses in our sin" to make us get the point. Going our own way provides sufficient consequences. But know this: as his son, he is only ever about his glory and your good. And part of getting us to joy in our marriage is through his discipline.

> *It is for discipline that you have to endure. God is treating you as sons. For what son is there whom his father does not discipline? For the moment all discipline seems painful rather than pleasant, but later it yields the peaceful fruit of righteousness to those who have been trained by it (Hebrews 12:7, 11).*

If you are desiring your relationship with your wife to look more like Jesus in full pursuit of his bride, if you are longing to be more of a visible man, I want to offer you three closing thoughts as we come to the end of this journey together. And I am already hearing some of the complaints that I hear from other guys: "Well, what about my wife? Is *she* not accountable for any change in her life? Why is everything about *me?*" Great question. And my response is this: God clearly calls *you,* as her husband, to lead and love your wife. He calls the *husband* to initiate. Of course, your wife is accountable for her responses, but if authentic change is going to come about in your marriage, it is going to demand the surrender of allowing God to get *your* heart posture where he desires it to be. Remember, you *cannot* control the responses of your wife, no matter how passionate your pleas nor how logical your reasonings. *Only God changes hearts.* And he wants you focused on your own sinfulness. Thomas Watson could not have said it better: "Until sin be bitter, Christ will not be sweet."[1] Then, and only then, are you ready, willing, and able to step into the life of your wife and serve her through humility and grace and grow your relationship. I am not guaranteeing that your repentance is going to save your marriage—God has to do that work, but if your marriage is going to change, you must start here.

So, what do you do next? You have read this book and come to the conclusion that your marriage needs help. But perhaps you are not sure what steps are needed to move you forward. Allow me to recap some of the ideas already presented in this book with some new ones. If you are committed to moving your marriage from where it is to where it should be, there are three foundational truths you must believe and embrace.

#1 YOU MUST HAVE A PROPER VIEW OF GOD

Messy marriages are hard to unravel when you are the one sitting in the mess. It feels like unraveling a ball of string full of tangles and knots. Where do you even begin? "Perhaps in ways that you have never come close to considering," Paul Tripp states, "your dissatisfaction is an awe problem."[2]

And herein lies the "Aha" moment for you: your dissatisfaction is ultimately sourced in your dissatisfaction of God. Though you may detest your own brokenness, though you may see your wife's sin as the bigger problem, your marriage is broken because your view of God is broken. We are either in awe of God or in awe of ourselves. There is no other option. And the sin that wreaks havoc in our marriages can most likely be traced to your awe of *your* agenda, *your* way, and *your* performance, which is the very reason you need Jesus and his gospel transforming your life. And if you are going to be truly changed in your heart, its affections, and its desires, then you must submit yourself to *God's* process for how change actually happens. As a friend has spoken to me, "You must see yourself as small and your sin as serious."

The truth is we *all* struggle in pursuing our wives like Jesus pursues his church. It is one of the many reasons I need a Savior because I make a horrible one. And perhaps you have been brought to that "God, I surrender" heart posture. But if you are like me, I have often tried to fix my marriage by using those magic words: "I'll do better and try harder next time." Exactly. It doesn't work. We then get discouraged over lack of change when the problem may be that we are not approaching change in a biblical manner.

So how *does* change happen? To foster biblically-genuine change demands that I go past surface layers and view the composition of my *heart*. And it demands asking questions. Much of our attempts at change are temporary because we fail to ask the better questions. So, allow me to present an example to you. Though this concept is not new, it really came alive for me on a leadership/backpacking trip through Pilgrimage where I leaned in as I learned about the "Transformation Cycle."

Your wife comes at you with a circumstance—word or action—that penetrates your heart in a foul way. Your reply is sarcastic, harsh, or defensive. Later, you realize what you did was sinful, and you want to make it right. Your inner conviction of "Why did I do that?" is met with an inner response of "I just need to keep my mouth shut next time and quit being sarcastic." Problem solved. But the most glaring issue is that you do not need the gospel for this type of temporary problem resolution. Authentic change demands Jesus. It demands a redemptive gospel that is active in our lives.

The "What do I need to do differently?" is many times the depth to which we look for change. But it is the wrong question or, at best, an incomplete question. God must help you understand your *heart* and its view of him. In the example above, when your wife ticked you off and your world was "out of balance," what were you expecting from her that you did not get? Was it respect? Significance? Or did you expect to be in control, and you clearly were not? These questions must be answered. But keep going, friend, because we must go deeper.

Why are respect, significance, or control so important to you? Why do you value these so highly? Many times what we are desiring is a *good* thing, but our thirst or longing for that thing soon turns it into an idol of the heart. Let's take the example of having to feel significant with your wife. This is what you value, so when you feel insignificant, you instinctively respond to your wife in a way that helps you feel significant. But here is a question for you: why do you have to feel significant when you are an adopted son of God, blessed in Christ with every spiritual blessing, chosen before the foundations of the world, holy and blameless before him in love (Ephesians 1)? Or let's use the example of your valuing being in control with your wife. If this is what you value, then when you feel you are not in control with your wife, you maneuver the situation to regain control. But why is control so important to you when God is sovereign in all aspects of your life and uses *all things* to help you be shaped into the image of his Son Jesus (Romans 8:28–29)? These are the types of questions that must be answered in order to expose the lies and hypocrisy of your heart. Sorry, I warned you this was not going to be easy. We have not gone deep enough though.

Why are respect, significance, or control *driving* you? You know, those deep-down, gut desires that feed the "kingdom of me." Until you get to the root level of what is driving you, you will get discouraged or frustrated because your attempts to change will only multiply in their frequency. Respect, significance, or control drive you because you have flawed views of God—of his character or his view of you—and what is important to you, what you value, and what drives you are the fruit of being in awe of yourself. And it is your creed or beliefs about God that you want God to address. Until you get to this level of questioning, you will never experience the freedom and joy that you so desire in your marriage. You will never have heart-level change.

Allow me to tie all of this together for you. Remember the story of me and my dad? My flawed view of God produced in me a fear of man and people pleasing. I did not believe at that time that God was bigger than my problem and that he was going to use it to make me look like Jesus. It was almost as if I saw God rolling his eyes at me—did he really care? God was small, so I had to step in and generate by own solutions. This wrong view of God became my driver in life and the lens through which I viewed my marriage. And because this drove me, I valued peace at all costs more than I loved God. It became easier for me to "fix" my wife than to deal with my root issues. So, what became important to me was to posture events and circumstances in a way that allowed me to be viewed favorably. It was important for *me* to maintain *control* in the situation and that included keeping my wife at arm's length from seeing what was really going on inside of me. And because that was important to me, I had expectations for how this part of our marriage needed to look, and when things felt out of control, I responded in a manner that I perceived was winning back control.

My ungodly responses to my wife were linked all the way back to my poor view of God. Unfortunately, when my wife and I talked about this, I believed my "Hey hon, I am sorry I did that" to be the catalyst for change, when in reality it was the catalyst for more failure. *God had to take me deeper* so that I could see how viewing him wrongly was the source of all of my brokenness. Until Jesus became my identity in my marriage, I scraped and clawed for what ended up being pitiful trinkets of my own making.

Let's go back to David and his sin with Bathsheba, his murder of Uriah, and the subsequent death of the child produced through David's affair. In Psalm 51, David's raw and transparent confession of his sin, he cries out to God, "Against you, you only, have I sinned and done what is evil in your sight." Didn't David grievously sin against Bathsheba and Uriah? Yes, but his sin was simply a fruit of his first and foremost poor view of God.

This is the level to which you must go, my friend. And until you do, your change will be impulsive and short-lived. We fear seeing our ugliness and its depths. I know that I do. But God wants to press us *through* that to see his beauty. And the more God drew me into Christ-centered worship, grace-wrought repentance, and a proper identity through the Scriptures, the more *he* grew his fruit of the Spirit within me. And its overflow was a humble heart, a quickness to repent, and an esteeming of the words of God. Once I saw God for who he was, I began to believe he was for my good and not evil. He wanted to be *the* rescue plan. Seeing God rightly led me to true confession and repentance for my unbelief and repentance to my wife. "I used to believe *this* about you, God, but now I believe *this!*"

God then put new desires and affections within me. These new affections replaced old thinking and created new drivers within me. Because I was driven by truth instead of error, I began to value openness and honesty with my wife. It was so difficult to carry out, but God pressed me through it. I began to value *her* over the protection of *me*. What then became important was our reconciliation and the freedom and joy that daily repentance brings. Ah, freedom. New values produced new expectations within me toward my wife, and it was not long before I was pursuing my wife more and I desired to serve her, help her reach her goals, and sanctify her. All of this has now produced new responses within me. I just do not feel this driving need to have to defend myself or display my "rightness" with her anymore, as one example. As with the apostle Paul, I recognize that my flesh still wants its way and my brokenness still manifests itself toward Stefanie. I am not where I want to be as a husband, but I am humbly grateful that I am not where I used to be. Jesus has done this because he can. To have *genuine* change demands embracing God's process for change and ceasing to follow your own flawed and deceived practices. *You must view him rightly.*

#2 YOU MUST ALLOW THE SCRIPTURES TO SHAPE YOUR VIEW OF GOD

Guys, this means we must be reading the Bible regularly. There is no other path to genuine change in our personal lives or in our marriages. It is our *hope.* Paul clearly reveals this in Romans 15:4. "For whatever was written in former days was written for our instruction, that through endurance and through the encouragement of the Scriptures we might have hope." Did you catch that? *Through the encouragement of the Scriptures we might have hope.*

And it is not enough to read a passage of Scripture to check it off our list. We must see Jesus in all of Scripture and seek how his gospel desires to transform our hearts *where they are at.* We are reminded in Hebrews 4:12: "For the word of God is living and active, sharper than any two-edged sword, piercing to the division of soul and of spirit, of joints and of marrow, and discerning the thoughts and intentions of the heart."

I believe much of our problem as guys is that we have missed the *entire* point of the Scriptures. And the point is this: they are not about *us!* They are about *Jesus.* He is the central theme of every page, and all of Scripture points to Him. But yet somehow, we have missed the Savior … *our* Savior. And Jesus could not have been more indicting of the Pharisees regarding this matter: "You search the Scriptures because you think that in them you have eternal life; and it is they that bear witness about me, yet you refuse to come to me that you may have life" (John 5:39–40).

Did you read that? There was no group more dedicated to reading the Scriptures than the Pharisees, and yet they missed the main character of Jesus! They read *about* Jesus and yet refused to submit themselves *to* Jesus. And men, reading our Bibles without seeing Jesus is only going to make us religiously self-righteous. Instead of loving and nurturing our wives, we end up becoming judgmental of them and view them as the greater sinner. And that is exactly what happened to the Pharisees. When reading God's Word becomes a requirement and we miss Jesus, we become convinced of our "doing" instead of our "being." And our subsequent failings will discourage us.

If you are not reading the Scriptures with Jesus as the main theme, the Bible is most likely boring to you, a series of random stories, and if you would be honest, irrelevant. But God can help you see beyond these characters to Jesus, who is the true and better character in every story. We can quickly skim over the story of Abraham offering Isaac as a sacrifice and fail to see Jesus as the true and better Isaac. As Abraham led his son to be sacrificed, there was another father who led his son up a hill to actually die for the sins of the people and to redeem a people for his glory. We can read the story of Joseph and be somewhat inspired about a young man who stayed faithful in the midst of betrayal yet became second in command, bringing hope to his people. Or we can see that this story points beyond Joseph to Jesus, who was rejected by his own people but used his position to free men and women from eternal slavery to sin. If Jesus is the true and better of every story, then the Bible is one consistent theme instead of a collection of unrelated stories.[3]

Do you recall after Jesus's resurrection how he walked with two disciples to the village of Emmaus? At first the two men did not recognize the risen Savior, but their hearts were intently drawn to his words. They told Jesus of all that had happened in Jerusalem in the last days. And as they neared the end of their journey, it says this about Jesus: "And beginning with Moses and all the Prophets, he interpreted to them in all the Scriptures the things concerning himself" (Luke 24:27).

Instead of simply reviewing more details of the last few days, Jesus took the time to explain the grand narrative of all of Scripture: himself. From Moses, the law, to the prophets, to their current day, Jesus revealed himself. The story of Jesus did not begin with his birth in Luke chapter 2. All of Scripture makes much of Jesus. He is the overarching theme. He is the main point.

It is Jesus's truth that transforms a heart, and that truth will pierce our hearts as the Holy Spirit helps us to see our true identity in Jesus. The Bible is so distinct because it contains things from God that we cannot understand in our own intellect. But this is the role of the Holy Spirit in our lives: "Now we have received not the spirit of the world, but the Spirit who is from God, that we might understand the things freely given us by God" (1 Corinthians 2:12).

The oft-forgotten member of the Trinity desires to reveal Jesus to you. He convinces us of our righteous standing before God and of the power of the gospel *through the Scriptures*. The Word of God is unparalleled in its ability to transform your heart. Read Psalm 119 and rehearse the myriad ways the Psalmist describes the effects of God's Word on his life:

"I have stored up your word in my heart, that I might not sin against you."

"Your word is a lamp to my feet and a light to my path."

"The sum of your word is truth, and every one of your righteous rules endures forever."

#3 YOU MUST SEEK OUT BIBLICAL COMMUNITY

"We are conditioned in countless ways to think and act as individuals only," Tim Keller states, "not as members of any body."[4] I am finding this especially true among men. I am not talking about the ability for guys to have a commonality in doing some hobby together or just "hanging out." I am referring to the lack of biblical community among guys who claim to be brothers in Christ.

It has become a lost art among many, and it cannot be replaced by other aspects of a relationship. If you are desiring your relationship with your wife to look different than it does, you must have a right view of God and allow the Scriptures to shape that view. But not only that, you must also have a biblical view of community. And I am not just referring to your wife—though you certainly need it there as well. I am referring to having community with other men.

What do I mean by biblical community? I define community as doing life with other men to more fully express the gospel and live out our identity in Jesus. It is a fighting side by side against the assaults of the enemy. It is designed for both mutual investment and mutual accountability. Allow me to give you an example from my own life. Tension enters the marital paradise of Antone and Stefanie. I can tend to resolve these situations by disengaging from my wife and counseling myself. I love counseling myself because I am actually very good at it. I can counsel myself into despair or pity within about forty-three seconds. My wife may not even know that I am struggling with something she said or did. But I have chosen to do this thing solo. We often justify our actions by attaching Christian words and telling ourselves we just need God to help us "process things." What I usually mean is that I want some dedicated time to rehearse the situation to convince myself why I am right and my wife is wrong.

As I tell my story to others, guys resonate that we are tempted to live life like we are paddling solo in a canoe, reading a washed-out map, and using a broken compass. Right now I am thinking of multiple guys whose marriages are a mess. In *every* scenario, the husband has not been in community with other guys about his struggles but rather has chosen to bear them alone. The husbands only chose to communicate with other guys when things exploded. I believe men struggle being in community with other men for three reasons: 1) they think their struggles and brokenness are unique to them, 2) they are embarrassed about their brokenness and their need for help, or 3) they believe they really do not need the help of other guys to foster change in their lives. To which I would reply 1) no, they are not, 2) get over yourself, and 3) you have bought into the lie. We have forgotten we are on mission ... together. Greg Morse *nailed* it:

> When the church is on mission, men, out of sheer necessity and love for their families and fellow man, will act more manfully. When the deception of peacetime is exposed, men will see snipers shooting at their brother through pornography. They will see missiles of worldliness fired at their children. They will see the serpent trying to entangle their wives in barbed wires. And they will see souls being lost daily under this present darkness. Their manliness will forbid passivity. They will button up the uniform and go to war.[5]

Community is doing life with other guys so that the gospel is mutually influencing us. Notice around what community is centered: the gospel. This demands that I am seeking out other men who are rooted and grounded in the truths of Jesus Christ and the identity we find in him. I need to be cautious because it is easy to say we have community when, in fact, it is only a group of husbands complaining about the woes of their marriages while other men chime in, "Oh yeah, me too, me too!" That is not biblical community. That is permission to continue being a poor example of a husband. It is not what I need, and it is not what you need. What every husband must have is a few other men in their lives where there is freedom and an expectation for going beyond the "How are you doing in your marriage? Fine" type conversations.

What does this look like? Here is a sample of the type of community that has occurred between myself and one of my brothers in the gospel. We were chatting in his truck one morning as we went to get some coffee. I was becoming concerned as I was not feeling well. I was having some physical discomfort in my chest, and it felt like stress. I was not sure what was going on. So, I started a conversation:

Me: "This is kind of random, but I am not feeling the best. I am starting to feel physical tension within me at times, and I do not know what is going on."

Brother: "You know, I have had that same type of thing happen to me. I am not sure, but I think you may want to see if there is anger going on somewhere in your life."

Me: "What? You think so?" (with a look of "Well, that can't be it.")

Brother: "Seriously. I have been feeling the same sort of response in me, and I am wondering if you need to check out if it is anger in your heart. I was given a powerful tool some time back. Go to the Psalm whose chapter matches the day of the month. Today is the tenth so go to Psalm 10. Then read every thirtieth chapter from your starting point until you have read five Psalms. Read them out loud and identify with the psalmist's thoughts and see how he works back to truth. It will be really helpful."

Me: "Okay, I will do that."

I had a solo strategic planning afternoon already scheduled and started with praying and reading those five Psalms. I really identified with David's cries of "Where are you God?" and begged God to reveal to me if anger might be at the root of my symptoms. And it was! He showed me that I was getting tense within when a plan of mine went awry or my agenda did not happen. I wanted control, and I was not getting it. What a freeing time of repentance and reconciliation I had with God. God used that casual conversation to peel back a layer of my heart that I was not seeing. And I am not saying every physical ailment is spiritually related, but I am highlighting the benefit that my own brokenness would not have been revealed and reconciliation gained were it not for having community.

And then there is time to be coached in the truths of the gospel. I get it: it can feel awkward because I am displaying my weakness and brokenness to another guy or my friend is talking about a side of him I had not seen before. How will they view me? How will I view them? What we discover is that we both are broken and that Jesus is the better solution. Actually, the *only* solution. We may be married to different women, but the foundational elements of conflict or struggle are common to every husband. And what is common is this: my sin will devastate my marriage, and there is no brokenness in my marriage that Jesus cannot heal. Once you get past that, conversations of this type become a part of what we do as one bro to another.

We must be convinced that community with other guys is not just a good idea but actually *essential.* Paul instructs the believers in Ephesus that ...

> *Rather, speaking the truth in love, we are to grow up in every way into him who is the head, into Christ, from whom the whole body, joined and held together by every joint with which it is equipped, when each part is working properly, makes the body grow so that it builds itself up in love (Ephesians 4:15–16).*

The metaphor displayed here is one of a body: Jesus is the head and we are its members. There are two things to notice in this passage. First, growth ultimately comes from Jesus. It is supernatural and not from our own efforts. Though these verses speak about all types of growth, change in our marriage certainly comes under that umbrella. Second, God has so structured the body that though change comes from the power of the Holy Spirit within us, he uses *us* to stir each other to love and good works. John Piper gives some excellent insights:

> *The second thing to see in verse 16 is that, even though the growth and building up of the body happens "from Christ," it is the body itself that is the immediate active cause of that growth. Verse 16: "... from whom the whole body ..." That's the subject of the sentence; now where is the verb? What does the whole body do? The verb is way down in the last line: "the whole body ... causes the growth of the body." Everything else in that verse explains how. But the basic sentence is "the whole body ... causes the growth of the body."*[6]

It really does not get any clearer than that. Too often we treat biblical community with other guys like an add-on when purchasing a car: "I want the leather seats, but I don't want the tinted windows." It is not a *suggestion* from God. It is a *commandment* because that is how God has designed growth—in community with other believers. So, do not be offended when I say that if you are not in community with other guys, you are in sin. Going solo in our spiritual growth does not work for believers in general, and it certainly will not work for a husband who desires to have a loving and healthy relationship with his wife.

I have had conversations where a brother who loves me has said, "You know, you may want to be careful about …" and proceeds to warn me about a mindset that I have taken into my relationship with Stefanie. Yes, it stings to have my sin pointed out, but on the back end I am so incredibly grateful to see what I was not seeing. The truth is that I don't know what I don't know, and I have blind spots in my life. Blind spots are labeled as such because I cannot see something going on in my life without the help of another.

Many of us are stuck in pornography, anger, lust, passivity, and being unloving, and our marriages are crumbling. "But I'll do better …" we tell ourselves, and we continue paddling our canoe on our own hoping that change will occur. But the truth is we are not isolated in canoes. Look around. Actually, we are all together on one big life raft going through similar issues and fighting similar battles. One of Satan's biggest ploys with husbands is to pick them off by confining them to their own thoughts. I have been there and periodically still go there. Discouragement, despondency, dread. These are the outcomes of fighting my battles alone.

"I *do* want that community with other men," you might say, "but I don't know how to get there." Here are a couple ideas that I would commend to you. 1) Talk with your pastor. Take him to lunch and be genuine about the state of your marriage. Your pastor plays an important role in your gospel-centered growth as a husband. Listen to his preaching and teaching. Seek him out for the hard questions. Ask for his insights and advice. He is there to help shepherd you. 2) Get the courage and go to lunch or coffee with a guy. Go through a book of the Bible together and see what God does in drawing your hearts together for battle.

But you will have to seek it out and be intentional. Most of the time, biblical community is not simply going to come to you. But community with other men is absolutely essential if you want to pursue your wife in a biblical way. It is not terribly difficult, and it may feel awkward at first. Press through it. Get comfortable with asking another guy, "So hey, how are you *really* doing in your marriage? What is God up to in your life?"

> When we are convinced that we stand in a war zone, invading a contested beach against spiritual forces of evil, we will not be content to only gather for the ballgame or work on home projects. We will meet to study God's Word. We will meet to pray together. We will meet to discuss our struggles, victories, aspirations, and ambitions. We will stay in contact throughout the week. We will strategize. We will help each other amputate limbs. We will speak hard truths to one another. We will laugh together. We will bleed together. We will survive together. Their struggles will become our struggles, and their souls will be part of our responsibility.[7]

A right view of God. Engaging the Scriptures. Seeking out community with other men. These are the cornerstones to building a thriving marriage and being a visible man.

So here is what you should be asking . . .

COMMUNION WITH GOD: Why is your poor view of God always at the root of the brokenness you exhibit toward your wife?

COMMUNICATION WITH YOUR WIFE: What are ways you and I can foster biblical community, both together and individually?

COMMUNITY WITH OTHER MEN: Let's talk through our biggest obstacles in loving our wives. How can we partner together to be "visible men"?

CONCLUSION

Husbands, love your wives, as Christ loved the church and gave himself up for her, that he might sanctify her, having cleansed her by the washing of water with the word, so that he might present the church to himself in splendor, without spot or wrinkle or any such thing, that she might be holy and without blemish (Ephesians 5:25–27).

So, we have come to the end. Where are you in all of this? How are *you* pursuing your wife? No really. Are you a visible man? Don't ignore or overlook these questions. Is your marriage truly a reflection of the more glorious reality of Jesus loving his church?

There is hope. And that hope is only in Jesus. I want you to quit feeling the pressures of performance and gritting it out to make your marriage work. I want you to understand that, if you are a son of God, you have the very same power within you that victoriously resurrected Jesus from the grave. Jesus can heal your marriage.

There is life. If you are at odds with your wife and sin has wielded its deceptively destructive hand in your marriage, know that Jesus can spring life out of your dying marriage. I am thankful for where my marriage is today with Stefanie, but it did not come because of haphazard choices in my life. It came because God broke me. He broke me and then remade me. And what I failed to believe was that God was not just after his glory but also after *my joy.*

Humility is a gift of the gospel. Repentance is a gift of the gospel. Reconciliation is a gift of the gospel. But God has called *you* as her husband to initiate these in your relationship through his power. It was not easy for me, and it will not be easy for you. But I would not trade anything for the renewed relationship I have with my wife. It has been spiritual warfare, but it has been worth it.

Jesus is better. He is better than your passivity, your lust, better than your feeling significant, or your striving for control. He is better than your disengaging, your having to be right, or your having the last word. He is better than *all* of these. "For our sake he made him to be sin who knew no sin, so that in him we might become the righteousness of God" (2 Corinthians 5:21). This is said about Jesus. Do you *believe* this about him? Do you *believe* that the righteousness of Jesus has been credited to you if you are a believer in the life, death, burial, and resurrection of Jesus?

I have openly shared glimpses into my marriage so that you can identify with my own struggles and the day-to-day messiness of being in a covenantal relationship. With all its ugliness and scars and brokenness, grace is winning out. And it makes me incredibly thankful that Jesus did not just observe my mess and bark out instructions, but he entered into it with me and mercifully led me out. And he still leads me out.

Marriage in full pursuit, looking like Jesus loving and serving his bride, is the only marriage that will yield the joy, peace, and harmony that you and your wife are seeking. It is all found in the life-breathing power of the gospel. Brokenness is still going to rear its ugly head, but reconciliation will be the primary quest. And understand this: God can actually take the brokenness in your life and use it for your benefit in looking like Jesus. He will actually grow you *because* of it, not in *spite* of it.

Beg God to do a work in you because that is where it is going to start. Ask him to change the affections and desires of your heart toward your bride and then watch him do it. But be patient. See him give back the fruitless years of your marriage. Experience a love in your relationship that will bring fulfillment and joy and most of all, glory to God. Ask God to transform you into a visible man.

NOTES

CHAPTER 1: IN FULL PURSUIT

1. John Piper, "Call Me Husband, Not Baal," *Desiring God,* March 24, 2018, www.desiringgod.org/messages/call-me-husband-not-baal#pursuing-an-unfaithful-wife.
2. Timothy Keller, et al, *The Meaning of Marriage: Facing the Complexities of Commitment with the Wisdom of God* (New York: Dutton, 2011), 44.
3. "Redeem, Redemption – Vine's Expository Dictionary of New Testament Words," *Blue Letter Bible,* accessed July 6, 2018, www.blueletterbible.org/search/Dictionary/viewTopic.cfm?topic=VT0002329.
4. James Orr, "Steward," *International Standard Bible Encyclopedia Online,* accessed August 20, 2018, www.internationalstandardbible.com/S/steward.html.

CHAPTER 2: RECALIBRATING MY VIEW OF GOD

1. A. W. Tozer, *Knowledge of the Holy: Knowing God Through His Attributes* (Zeeland: Reformed Church Publications, 2018), 4.
2. "Isaiah 66:2 (KJV)," *Blue Letter Bible,* accessed July 6, 2018, www.blueletterbible.org/lang/Lexicon/Lexicon.cfm?strongs=H5027&t=KJV.
3. Andrew Murray, *Humility* (Nashville: B & H Publishing Group, 2017), 4.
4. John Stott, "Pride, Humility & God," *Sovereign Grace Online,* September/

October 2000, http://www.sovereigngraceministries.org/sgo/v18no5/prt_
pride.html (site discontinued).

5. Jerry Bridges, *Respectable Sins: Confronting the Sins We Tolerate* (Colorado
Springs: NavPress, 2007), 9.

6. "Isaiah 66:2 (KJV)," *Blue Letter Bible,* accessed July 6, 2018, www.
blueletterbible.org/lang/Lexicon/Lexicon.cfm?strongs=H5223&t=KJV.

7. Kevin DeYoung, *Just Do Something: a Liberating Approach to Finding God's
Will* (Chicago: Moody Publishers, 2014), 65.

8. "Psalm 139:23 (KJV)," *Blue Letter Bible,* accessed July 6, 2018, www.
blueletterbible.org/lang/Lexicon/Lexicon.cfm?strongs=H3045&t=KJV.

CHAPTER 3: WHEN MY IDENTITY DERAILS ME

1. John Piper, "Christian Identity and Christian Destiny," *Desiring God,* March
24, 2018, www.desiringgod.org/messages/christian-identity-and-christian-
destiny.

2. "John 15:2 (KJV)," *Blue Letter Bible,* accessed July 6, 2018, www.
blueletterbible.org/lang/Lexicon/Lexicon.cfm?strongs=G2508&t=KJV.

3. "John 16 Commentary – Matthew Henry Commentary on the Whole Bible
(Complete)," *Bible Study Tools,* accessed July 6, 2018, www.biblestudytools.
com/commentaries/matthew-henry-complete/john/16.html.

CHAPTER 4: THE FOUR ESSENTIALS OF HUSBANDING

1. "Make a Man Out of You Lyrics from Mulan," *Disney Clip Art Galore -
All-Original Disney and Pixar Images,* accessed November 20, 2018, www.
disneyclips.com/lyrics/lyrics37.html <http://www.disneyclips.com/lyrics/
lyrics37.html>.

2. Nicola Menzie, "Philly Pastor Eric Mason Talks 'Cultural Crisis' of
Manhood," *The Christian Post,* Christian Post, May 4, 2013, www.
christianpost.com/news/philly-pastor-eric-mason-talks-cultural-crisis-of-
manhood-95239/.

3. Robert Lewis, *Raising a Modern-Day Knight* (Carol Stream: Tyndale House
Publishers, 2007), 51–60.

4. John Piper, "For Men: What the Life of Augustine Teaches Us," *Desiring*

God, August 20, 2018, www.desiringgod.org/articles/for-men-what-the-life-of-augustine-teaches-us.

5. C. K. Chesterton and Robert Blaisdell, *G. K. Chesterton Quotes* (Mineola: Dover Publications, 2015), 32.

6. "Hebrews 4:16 (KJV)," *Blue Letter Bible,* accessed July 6, 2018, www.blueletterbible.org/lang/Lexicon/Lexicon.cfm?strongs=G3954&t=KJV.

CHAPTER 6: MARRIAGE UNDER CONTRACT

1. "IMarriage 2: Putting Your I Out," September 17, 2013, www.youtube.com/watch?v=dpD_V8-hrSk.

2. "IMarriage 2: Putting Your I Out," September 17, 2013, www.youtube.com/watch?v=dpD_V8-hrSk.

3. "Ephesians 5:31 (KJV)," *Blue Letter Bible,* accessed July 6, 2018, www.blueletterbible.org/lang/Lexicon/Lexicon.cfm?strongs=G4347&t=KJV.

CHAPTER 7: THE LENS OF FORBEARANCE AND GRACE

1. "Redeemed Lyrics," *Lyrics.com <http://Lyrics.com>,* accessed December 2, 2018, www.lyrics.com/lyric/26143660/Big+Daddy+Weave/Redeemed <http://www.lyrics.com/lyric/26143660/Big+Daddy+Weave/Redeemed>.

2. David T. Harvey, *When Sinners Say "I Do": Discovering the Power of the Gospel for Marriage* (Wapwallopen: Shepherd Press, 2011), 81.

3. Harvey, 88.

4. Harvey, 88.

5. Harvey, 88.

6. "Luke 7:39 (KJV)," *Blue Letter Bible,* accessed July 6, 2018, www.blueletterbible.org/lang/Lexicon/Lexicon.cfm?strongs=G268&t=KJV.

7. Harvey, 88.

8. Milton Vincent, *A Gospel Primer: for Christians* (Bemidjii: Focus Publishing, 2008), 24–25.

CHAPTER 8: THE HOLY INTIMACY IN MARRIAGE

1. John Piper, *This Momentary Marriage: A Parable of Permanence* (Wheaton: Crossway, 2012), 127–128.

2. Dennis Rainey, *Preparing for Marriage: Discover God's Plan for a Lifetime of Love* (Bloomington: Bethany House, 2010), 218.

3. Piper, 133.

4. Piper, 134.

5. "1 Peter 3:7 (KJV)," *Blue Letter Bible,* accessed July 6, 2018, www.blueletterbible.org/lang/Lexicon/Lexicon.cfm?strongs=G4924&t=KJV.

CHAPTER 9: GETTING THERE

1. Thomas Watson, *Doctrine of Repentance* (Edinburgh: Banner of Truth Trust, reprinted 1987), 63.

2. Paul D. Tripp, *Awe: Why It Matters for Everything We Think, Say, and Do* (Wheaton: Crossway, 2015), 20.

3. Justin Taylor, "Keller: Gospel-Centered Ministry," *The Gospel Coalition,* May 23, 2007, www.thegospelcoalition.org/blogs/justin-taylor/keller-gospel-centered-ministry/.

4. Tim Keller, "The Difficulty of Community – Redeemer Report," *Redeemer Churches and Ministries,* October 2009, www.redeemer.com/redeemer-report/article/the_difficulty_of_community.

5. Greg Morse, "Men Under Fire: Why We Need Male Friends," *Desiring God,* July 6, 2018, www.desiringgod.org/articles/men-under-fire.

6. Piper, John, "How Christ Enables the Church to Upbuild Itself in Love," *Desiring God,* March 24, 2018, www.desiringgod.org/messages/how-christ-enables-the-church-to-upbuild-itself-in-love.

7. Morse.